W9-AQS-769

# N O T E S™

# ETHICAL AND LEGAL ASPECTS OF NURSING

**Joseph T. Catalano, RN, PhD, CCRN**

Dr. Catalano, author of this book, is an Associate Professor of Nursing at East Central University, Ada, Oklahoma. He received a Bachelor of Arts degree in Philosophy from St. Hyacinth College, Granby, Massachusetts; his Diploma in Nursing from St. Elizabeth School of Nursing, Utica, New York; his BSN from the State University Of New York at Utica/Rome; his MSN from the State University of New York at Buffalo; and his PhD in Higher Education from the University of North Texas, Denton. Dr. Catalano is a member of the American Nurses' Association and the American Association of Critical Care Nurses. He serves as Vice-President of the Oklahoma Nurses' Association, District 10, and is a board member of the American Diabetic Association of Oklahoma.

**Susan Griffin, RN, MSN, MA**

Ms. Griffin, reviewer of this book, is an Associate Professor of Nursing Education at Palomar College, San Marcos, California. She received her Diploma in Nursing from Queen of Angels School of Nursing, Los Angeles; her BSN from San Diego State University; her MSN from California State University, Los Angeles; and her MA in Educational Technology from San Diego State University. Ms. Griffin is a member of the National League for Nursing and the Southern California Nursing Diagnosis Association.

Springhouse Corporation
Springhouse, Pennsylvania

# Staff

**Executive Director, Editorial**
Stanley Loeb

**Director of Trade and Textbooks**
Minnie B. Rose, RN, BSN, MEd

**Art Director**
John Hubbard

**Senior Acquisitions Editor**
Susan L. Mease

**Clinical Consultant**
Maryann Foley, RN, BSN

**Editor**
David Moreau

**Copy Editor**
Mary Hohenhaus Hardy

**Designers**
Stephanie Peters (associate art director),
Susan Hopkins Rodzewich

**Art Production**
Robert Perry (manager), Heather Bernhardt,
Anna Brindisi, Donald Knauss, Tom Robbins,
Robert Wieder

**Typography**
David Kosten (director), Diane Paluba (manager),
Elizabeth Bergman, Joyce Rossi Biletz, Phyllis
Marron, Robin Rantz, Valerie Rosenberger

**Manufacturing**
Deborah Meiris (manager), T.A. Landis,
Jennifer Suter

**Production Coordination**
Aline S. Miller (manager), Maura Murphy

**Library of Congress Cataloging-in-Publication Data**

Catalano, Joseph T.
Ethical and legal aspects of nursing / Joseph T. Catalano, author; Susan Griffin, reviewer.
  p. cm. — (Springhouse notes)
  Includes bibliographical references.
  Includes index.
  ISBN 0-87434-315-1
  1. Nursing—Law and legislation—United States—Outlines, syllabi, etc. 2. Nursing—Moral and ethical aspects—Outlines, syllabi, etc.
  I. Griffin, Susan, 1942- . II. Title. III. Series.
  [DNLM: 1. Ethics, Nursing. 2. Legislation, Nursing. 3. Malpractice—nurses' instruction. WY 85 C357e]
KF2915.N8C37      1991
344.73'0414—dc20
[347.304414]
DNLM/DLC                              90-10230

# Contents

# How to Use Springhouse Notes

Today, more than ever, nursing students face enormous time pressures. Nursing education has become more sophisticated, increasing the difficulties students have with studying efficiently and keeping pace.

The need for a comprehensive, well-designed series of study aids is great, which is why we've produced Springhouse Notes...to meet that need. Springhouse Notes provide essential course material in outline form, enabling the nursing student to study more effectively, improve understanding, achieve higher test scores, and get better grades.

Key features appear throughout each book, making the information more accessible and easier to remember.
- **Learning Objectives.** These objectives precede each section in the book to help the student evaluate knowledge before and after study.
- **Key Points.** Highlighted in color throughout the book, these points provide a way to quickly review critical information. Key points may include:
  —a cardinal sign or symptom of a disorder
  —the most current or popular theory about a topic
  —a distinguishing characteristic of a disorder
  —the most important step of a process
  —a critical assessment component
  —a crucial nursing intervention
  —the most widely used or successful therapy or treatment.
- **Points to Remember.** This information, found at the end of each section, summarizes the section in capsule form.
- **Glossary.** Difficult, frequently used, or sometimes misunderstood terms are defined for the student at the end of each section.

**Remember:** Springhouse Notes are learning tools designed to *help* you. They are not intended for use as a primary information source. They should never substitute for class attendance, text reading, or classroom note-taking.

This book, *Ethical and Legal Aspects of Nursing,* uses ethical theories and concepts as a framework for examining ethical decision making and ethical issues in nursing. The book then explores the origins of law and the judicial system to introduce various legal aspects of nursing: ethical codes, nurse practice acts, criminal and civil liabilities, and licensure, among others. The book concludes with detailed, informative sections on legally sensitive practice settings and specific suggestions for all nurses who want to avoid legal jeopardy.

# Overview of Ethics and Law in Nursing

**Learning Objectives**
After studying this section, the reader should be able to:

● Define the key terms used in ethics and law.

● Identify significant trends in society and health care that have affected current ethical and legal issues.

● Describe professional accountability and discuss its implications for the nurse.

## I. Overview of Ethics and Law in Nursing

### A. Terms used in ethics and law

1. Values
   a. *Values* are concepts or ideals that give meaning to one's life and provide a framework for one's decisions and actions
   b. Values usually are associated with individuals rather than groups and can include religious beliefs, sexual orientation, family relationships, prejudices, and roles
   c. *Value conflicts* can arise when events force one to act against one's beliefs (for instance, a nurse who is religiously opposed to abortion may be assigned to care for a patient who has had an abortion)

2. Morals
   a. *Morals* are the standards of right and wrong that one learns through socialization
   b. Morals usually are based on religious beliefs
   c. Morals usually are associated with individuals or small groups
   d. Morals are manifested as behavior in accord with a group's customs or tradition

3. Ethics
   a. *Ethics* are systems of valued behaviors and beliefs that govern proper conduct to ensure the protection of an individual's rights
   b. Ethics involve judgments that help to differentiate right from wrong or indicate how things ought to be
   c. Ethics are associated with individuals, small groups, or society

4. Ethical code
   a. An *ethical code* is a written list of a profession's values and standards of conduct
   b. An ethical code provides a framework for decision making
   c. An ethical code undergoes periodic revision to reflect changes in society and the profession
   d. An ethical code usually exceeds — but never falls short of — the boundaries established by law
   e. Each professional is responsible for upholding the values and standards established in the ethical code
   f. An ethical code usually is unenforceable

5. Statements of etiquette
   a. *Statements of etiquette* describe expected professional behaviors established in ethical codes
   b. Statements of etiquette focus on protecting a professional's rights rather than an individual's rights; for example, one such statement in the medical code of ethics focuses on a doctor's right to refuse to treat patients

6. Laws
   a. *Laws* are rules of social conduct designed to prevent the actions of one party from infringing on the rights of another party
   b. Laws are necessary within social groups
   c. Laws are enforceable
7. Human rights
   a. *Human rights* are the set of entitlements that one deserves according to just claim, legal guarantees, or moral principles
   b. Rights can originate from natural law, such as the right to live, or from legal assignment by the government, such as those rights of privacy and liberty that are guaranteed by the Constitution
   c. Based on the strict definition of rights, health care is probably a privilege rather than a right
   d. Health care professionals, however, may view health care as an individual's right rather than a privilege because they typically feel an obligation to provide care

**B. Historical trends**
   1. 1850-1939
      a. Neither the public nor health care professionals showed much concern for ethical issues in nursing and health care
      b. Few malpractice cases were litigated, and consumer involvement in health care was minimal
      c. The U.S. government had few standards and regulations to guide health care and nursing
      d. The public did not consider nursing to be a profession and therefore did not hold it to high standards
      e. *Health care paternalism* resulted in a limited concept of informed consent
      f. Medical and nursing interventions had little success in curing serious diseases or prolonging life
      g. Health care was technologically unsophisticated, relying heavily on personal contact between the sick and the health care provider
   2. 1940 to the present
      a. World War II caused a significant increase in the use of surgery and life-support equipment in health care
      b. The development of antibiotics, psychotropic medications, and other technological advances vastly improved the medical community's ability to treat injuries, cure illnesses, and save lives
      c. Nursing became more skill-oriented to deal with advances in medical technology and to enhance the life-saving effects of medicine
      d. Increased media coverage of advances in medical technology and services led to greater expectations of success by the public
      e. Gradually, society came to perceive advanced medical care as a right rather than a privilege

    f. As nursing and health care became more skill-oriented, the treatment of patients became less personalized

    g. The public began to perceive the health sciences as infallible and health care as a person-to-institution relationship; consequently, patients were more inclined to use litigation as a means of retribution for harm resulting from treatments

    h. Increased medical specialization fragmented health care into many subservices

    i. Government scandals, such as the Watergate episode, intensified public mistrust of institutions and encouraged scrutiny of other service institutions, including hospitals and nursing homes

    j. Increased public involvement in consumer organizations led to higher ethical and health care standards

    k. Increased governmental regulation of health care led to more stringent standards and guidelines for health care institutions

    l. Health care practitioners have sometimes failed to recognize the ethical and legal implications of their actions, perhaps because they have been trained to act first and review the consequences later and because they have traditionally mistrusted the legal system

    m. Health care providers have begun to develop ethical codes in response to such issues as the rights of patients, the competency of health care providers, and the responsibilities of health care institutions

    n. Laws and ethical codes have been unable to keep pace with advances in science and health care, creating ethical crises and difficult legal questions

## C. Professional accountability in nursing

1. General information

    a. *Accountability* means answerability or responsibility

    b. Nurses, as professionals, are responsible for their actions

    c. Accountability in nursing comprises *personal accountability* (to oneself and to the patient) and *public accountability* (to the employer and to society)

    d. The primary goals of professional accountability in nursing are to maintain high standards of care and to protect the patient from harm

    e. Licensure creates a legal basis for professional accountability in nursing

2. Personal accountability

    a. Nurses are accountable to themselves for proper use of their knowledge and skills in providing care

    b. Nurses are accountable to the patient because the patient is dependent on nurses for care

    c. Nurses must be aware of and responsible for each action taken or decision made, be able to defend it, and be willing to accept the consequences

    d. Personal accountability increases with the degree of autonomy; the higher the degree of autonomy of actions, the greater the accountability

3. Public accountability
   a. Nurses are accountable to the employer because the institution pays their salary and allows them to practice as professionals
   b. Nurses are accountable to society because of its power to determine ethical rules and impose penalties for violating those rules and because each patient is a member of society
   c. The public's trust in a profession increases proportionately to the degree in which the profession's members guard and protect the public's interests
   d. Conflicts can arise when the nurse's obligations to the employer contradict her obligations to society's health needs

4. Implications for nurses
   a. To develop and evaluate new professional practices and to reevaluate existing ones
   b. To maintain professional goals and standards
   c. To provide time for self-reflection, ethical thought, and personal growth
   d. To increase the profession's reliability
   e. To establish boundaries for professional accountability by using ethical codes

## Points to Remember

Scientific and technological advances have led to a gradual depersonalization of health care.

Individuals are more likely to seek legal means to settle disputes about health care than they were in the past.

The public has high expectations of the health care system.

All professionals are responsible for their actions.

Professional nursing accountability protects the public, not the professional, and includes accountability to oneself, to the patient, to the employer, and to society.

## Glossary

**Health care paternalism** — belief that health care professionals know what is best for the patient and that the patient need not question the nature of care provided

**Informed consent** — patient's uncoerced permission to have a test or procedure performed after having been given complete information about the test or procedure, other options, and potential consequences of all choices

**Litigation** — act or process of taking a legal case to court

**Value conflicts** — incompatibilities or inconsistencies in beliefs, ideals, or concepts that arise within an individual when faced with opposing choices of action or between an individual and an institution when they hold opposing concepts of expected actions

# Ethical Theories

**Learning Objectives**

After studying this section, the reader should be able to:

- Discuss the major ethical theories used in decision making.

- Explain the key ideas and limitations of each ethical theory.

- Identify the ethical theory most appropriate for decision making in health care.

## II. Ethical Theories

### A. Introduction
1. Ethical theories attempt to provide a system of principles and rules for resolving ethical dilemmas
   a. An *ethical dilemma* is a situation that requires a decision to be made between two equally unfavorable or disagreeable alternatives
   b. Many health care decisions involve ethical dilemmas that have no clear-cut answers
2. Ethical theories consist of fundamental beliefs about what is morally right or wrong and propose reasons for maintaining these beliefs
3. Ethical theories provide the bases for professional codes of ethics

### B. Deontology
1. General information
   a. *Deontology* is a theory of ethical decision making based on the discovery and confirmation of a set of morals or rules that govern the resolution of ethical dilemmas
   b. Deontology attempts to determine what is right or wrong based on one's duty or obligation to act rather than on the action's consequences
   c. Because it emphasizes duty or obligation to another person, deontology is the only acceptable theory for ethical decision making in health care
   d. Immanuel Kant's Categorical Imperative, which asserts that all people should be respected and treated as ends rather than as means to an end, is a prime example of deontology
2. Key ideas
   a. Deontology is based on unchanging and absolute principles derived from universal values at the heart of all major religions
   b. Its basic principle is to ensure survival of the species by fulfilling one's duty or obligation to another person
   c. Any act in accord with one's duty or obligation is right, and any act not in accord with one's duty or obligation is wrong
3. Limitations
   a. Duties or obligations may conflict, requiring decisions about which duty or obligation takes precedence over another
   b. Questions commonly arise about the origin of a duty or obligation, such as "Who determined the duty?" or "Who identified the obligation?"
   c. Deontology can be inflexible

### C. Teleology
1. General information
   a. *Teleology* is a theory of ethical decision making that determines right or wrong based on an action's consequences
   b. Teleology is sometimes called *situation ethics* or *calculus morality*
   c. The principle of utility is the basis for teleology

    d. *Utilitarianism* is a teleological theory that judges acts based on their usefulness; useful acts bring about good, and useless acts bring about harm

2. Key ideas
   a. *Good* is defined as happiness or pleasure
   b. *Right* is defined as the greatest amount of good and the least amount of harm for the greatest number of people
   c. Teleology has no strict principles, moral codes, duties, or rules to determine conduct in particular situations
   d. A basic assumption is that good and harm can be quantified, as in a mathematical formula, so that one can evaluate the degree of good and evil in a specific case
   e. The decision maker judges actions in terms of their consequences for the general welfare if all people acted in a similar manner in the same situation

3. Limitations
   a. Some theorists contend that teleology advocates the maximum happiness of a few rather than the average happiness of all
   b. Because utility is the only principle one can use to determine whether an act is right or wrong, many conflicts go unresolved
   c. Questions usually arise about which is better — to produce the greatest amount of good or the least amount of harm for all
   d. Teleology tends to ignore the individual's rights and needs
   e. Quantifying the relative good and harm of actions, particularly in health care, is usually difficult if not impossible
   f. Determining the "greatest good" is highly subjective and can result in inconsistent decisions

**D. Egoism**
1. General information
   a. *Egoism* is a theory of ethical decision making that considers self-interest and self-preservation as the only proper goals of all human actions
   b. Egoism is based on the innate and primitive human tendency to be self-centered
2. Key ideas
   a. Egoism is based on the principle that the only right decision is the one that maximizes the pleasure of the decision maker
   b. Something is good and right if the individual desires it
   c. The decision maker in an ethical dilemma makes decisions based on personal comfort
3. Limitations
   a. Egoism does not consider moral principles or rules outside the individual's point of view
   b. Inconsistencies arise from one decision to the next, even in similar situations

      c. Social chaos can result when individuals act solely in their own interests
      d. Because it does not consider the rights of others, egoism is unacceptable for most decisions involving ethical situations in health care

## E. Obligationism
  1. General information
     a. *Obligationism* is a theory of ethical decision making that attempts to resolve ethical dilemmas by balancing *distributive justice* (dividing equally among all citizens) with *beneficence* (doing good and not harm)
     b. Obligationism is aimed primarily at public policymakers to encourage them to choose the best course of action for their citizens
  2. Key ideas
     a. In making decisions, one should promote or do what is good and prevent or eliminate what is harmful or evil
     b. Benefits and burdens should be distributed equally throughout society
     c. All people must be treated according to their merits and needs
  3. Limitations
     a. The two basic principles of obligationism—justice and beneficence—may conflict in certain situations
     b. The theory can be useful for determining public policy but holds little practicality for making decisions that will affect one person
     c. Obligationism provides little guidance for solving specific ethical dilemmas faced by the health care provider

## F. Social contract theory
  1. General information
     a. Social contract theory is based on the concept of *original position*
     b. The least advantaged persons in society (such as children or handicapped persons) are considered the norm
     c. Whether an act is right or wrong is determined from the norm's point of view
  2. Key ideas
     a. Social contract theory is based on the principle of distributive justice
     b. The "primary goods" (income, wealth, liberty, opportunity, and self-respect) must be distributed equally
     c. Each person has equal right to the greatest degree of liberty possible for all persons
     d. Social inequalities should be eliminated by giving the most to the least advantaged
  3. Limitations
     a. The theory lacks specific guidelines, which limits its usefulness in day-to-day health care decisions
     b. Social inequalities are impossible to eliminate

## Points to Remember

Deontology is the only acceptable ethical theory for decision making in health care because it emphasizes duty or obligation to another person.

Teleology judges acts based on their usefulness.

Egoism judges acts based on the degree of pleasure they give to the decision maker.

Obligationism and social contract theory judge acts based on the principle of distributive justice.

The most effective resolutions of ethical dilemmas are made within the framework of principles and rules that govern human contact.

## Glossary

**Beneficence** — promotion of good and prevention of harm

**Calculus morality** — attempt to quantify or weigh the social harm and benefits that would result from a given action in order to make an ethical decision

**Distributive justice** — principle that advocates equal allocation of benefits and burdens to all members of society

**Original position** — underlying principle of the social contract theory, which states that people in a society determine the principles of justice by which all members are bound to live

**Situation ethics** — teleological theory that judges acts based on predictable consequences

# Ethical Decision Making

**Learning Objectives**

After studying this section, the reader should be able to:

- Identify factors that influence ethical decision making.

- Explain the four concepts central to ethical decision making: autonomy, justice, fidelity, and benficence.

- Discuss the American Nurses' Association and International Council of Nurses codes for nurses.

- State the key rights outlined by the American Hospital Association's bill of rights for patients.

- Describe the importance of ethics to the nursing profession.

- Explain how a nurse makes an ethical decision.

## III. Ethical Decision Making

### A. Introduction

1. Decisions about ethical dilemmas are influenced by numerous and wide-ranging factors
2. As the world changes, new ethical dilemmas arise and old ethical dilemmas take on new significance
3. Major advances in science, technology, and health care during the past 50 years have outpaced the abilities of those in ethics and law to solve problems created by these advances

### B. Factors that influence ethical decision making in health care

1. Ethical decision making in health care has been influenced by numerous factors, including sociocultural changes, scientific and technological advances, legal issues, changes in the occupational status of health care workers, and consumer involvement in health care
2. Sociocultural factors have included:
   a. Attitudes about women and women's roles
   b. Beliefs and practices related to marriage and the family
   c. Increased emphasis on individual rights
   d. Religious values
   e. Values that society places on life and the right to die with dignity
   f. Demographic changes, such as increases in the number of poor and elderly clients in the population
   g. Availability of government funds for health care
3. Scientific and technological advances have included:
   a. Intensive care units
   b. Patient monitoring devices
   c. Life-sustaining medications
   d. Artificial life-support systems
   e. Renal dialysis
   f. Organ transplantation and artificial organs
   g. Computerized diagnostic equipment, such as the computerized tomography scan and magnetic resonance imaging
4. Legal issues have included:
   a. Abortion
   b. Adoption and baby selling
   c. In vitro fertilization
   d. Surrogate motherhood
   e. Right to die
   f. Right to refuse care
5. Changes in the occupational status of health care workers have included:
   a. Expanded roles, responsibilities, and educational requirements for nurses
   b. Collective bargaining and strikes
   c. More authoritarian attitude shown by hospitals toward their employees
   d. Attempts by nurses to increase their independence in practice

6. Consumer involvement in health care has led to:
   a. Demands by the public for a greater voice in health care decisions in response to a growing perception that health care has become depersonalized
   b. Establishment of ethics committees in hospitals to help guide health care practices
   c. Assumption by nurses of the role of consumer advocate
   d. Increased support and recognition of nurses from consumer groups

## C. Ethical concepts and ethical codes in decision making

1. Ethical decision making usually involves at least one of four basic concepts: autonomy, justice, fidelity, and beneficence
2. *Autonomy* refers to the right to make decisions about one's health care
   a. Autonomy has certain limitations, particularly when it interferes with another's rights
   b. Professionals also have a degree of autonomy
3. *Justice* refers to the obligation to be fair to all people
   a. This obligation applies to persons and governments
   b. The rights of one person become limited when they infringe on the rights of another person
4. *Fidelity* refers to one's faithfulness or loyalty to agreements and responsibilities that one has accepted
   a. Fidelity is one of the key elements of accountability
   b. Conflicts can arise between fidelity to patients and fidelity to employers, government, and society
5. *Beneficence* refers to the obligation to do good and not harm
   a. Problems can arise not only when trying to decide what is good for another person but also when determining who should make the decision
   b. A temporary harm to a patient may eventually produce a greater good during the course of treatment
6. Ethical decision making is based on ethical codes that serve as guidelines for the profession
   a. Ethical codes are based in part on the four concepts of autonomy, justice, fidelity, and beneficence
   b. Ethical codes are not static rules but rather dynamic guidelines that evolve to mirror changes in the profession and society
   c. Ethical codes in nursing outline the nurse's responsibilities to the patient, to the employer, and to society

## D. American Nurses' Association (ANA) Ethical Code for Nurses

1. General information
   a. The ANA Ethical Code for Nurses is the official statement of the national nurses' association for the United States (see *American Nurses' Association Ethical Code for Nurses*)
   b. The ANA code, developed in 1976, addresses specific health care issues and does not limit itself to statements of etiquette or broad general statements

   c.  The ANA code focuses on protecting the patient's rights while honoring obligations to the nursing profession and to the public

2. Key ideas
   a. Respect for human dignity
   b. Patient's right to privacy and confidentiality
   c. Patient and public safety
   d. Responsibility and accountability of nurses
   e. Nursing competency
   f. Participation in research
   g. Quality of patient care
   h. Nursing's integrity
   i. Collaboration with other members of the health care team

## AMERICAN NURSES' ASSOCIATION ETHICAL CODE FOR NURSES

The code is based upon beliefs about the nature of individuals, nursing, health, and society. Recipients and providers of nursing services are viewed as individuals and groups who possess basic rights and responsibilities, and whose values and circumstances command respect at all times. Nursing encompasses the promotion and restoration of health, the prevention of illness, and the alleviation of suffering. The statements of the code and their interpretation provide guidance for conduct and relationships in carrying out nursing responsibilities consistent with the ethical obligations of the profession and quality in nursing care.

- The nurse provides services with respect for human dignity and the uniqueness of the client unrestricted by considerations of social or economic status, personal attributes, or the nature of health problems.

- The nurse safeguards the client's right to privacy by judiciously protecting information of a confidential nature.

- The nurse acts to safeguard the client and the public when health care and safety are affected by the incompetent, unethical, or illegal practice of any person.

- The nurse assumes responsibility and accountability for individual nursing judgments and actions.

- The nurse maintains competence in nursing.

- The nurse exercises informed judgment and uses individual competence and qualifications as criteria in seeking consultation, accepting responsibilities, and delegating nursing activities to others.

- The nurse participates in activities that contribute to the ongoing development of the profession's body of knowledge.

- The nurse participates in the profession's efforts to implement and improve standards of nursing.

- The nurse participates in the profession's efforts to establish and maintain conditions of employment conducive to high-quality nursing care.

- The nurse participates in the profession's effort to protect the public from misinformation and misrepresentation and to maintain the integrity of nursing.

- The nurse collaborates with members of the health professions and other citizens in promoting community and national efforts to meet the health needs of the public.

### E. Canadian Nurses Association (CNA) Code of Ethics
1. General information
   a. The CNA Code of Ethics is the official statement of the national nurses' association for Canada (see *Canadian Nurses Association Code of Ethics*)

## CANADIAN NURSES ASSOCIATION CODE OF ETHICS

The body of the code is divided into the following sources of nursing obligations:

| | |
|---|---|
| **Clients** | • A nurse is obliged to treat clients with respect for their individual needs and values.<br>• Based on respect for clients and regard for their rights to control their own care, nursing care should reflect respect for clients' right of choice.<br>• The nurse is obliged to hold confidential all information about clients learned in the health care setting.<br>• The nurse has an obligation to be guided by consideration for the dignity of clients.<br>• The nurse is obligated to provide competent care to clients.<br>• The nurse is obliged to represent the ethics of nursing before colleagues and others.<br>• The nurse is obliged to advocate clients' interests.<br>• In all professional settings, including education, research, and administration, the nurse retains a commitment to the welfare of clients. The nurse has an obligation to act in a fashion that will maintain trust in nurses and nursing. |
| **Health team** | • Client care should represent a cooperative effort, drawing on the expertise of nursing and other health professions. By acknowledging personal or professional limitations, the nurse recognizes the perspective and expertise of colleagues from other disciplines.<br>• The nurse, as a member of the health care team, is obliged to take steps to ensure that clients receive competent and ethical care. |
| **Social context of nursing** | • Conditions of employment should contribute to client care and to the professional satisfaction of nurses. Nurses are obliged to work toward securing and maintaining conditions of employment that satisfy these goals. |
| **Responsibilities of the profession** | • Professional nurses' organizations recognize a responsiblity to clarify, secure, and sustain ethical nursing conduct. The fulfillment of these tasks requires professional organizations to remain responsive to the rights, needs, and interests of clients and nurses. |

From Canadian Nurses Association Code of Ethics for Nursing, 1985.

    b. This code of ethics was first published in 1980

    c. It addresses patients, the health care team, the social context of nursing, and the responsibilities of the profession

2. Key ideas

    a. Competency

    b. Respect and dignity

    c. Confidentiality

    d. Patient advocacy

    e. Coordination and collaboration

    f. Professional accountability

---

## INTERNATIONAL COUNCIL OF NURSES CODE OF ETHICS FOR NURSES

The fundamental responsibility of the nurse is fourfold: to promote health, to prevent illness, to restore health, and to alleviate suffering.

The need for nursing is universal. Inherent in nursing is respect for life, dignity, and rights of man. It is unrestricted by considerations of nationality, race, creed, color, age, sex, politics, or social status.

Nurses render health services to the individual, the family, and the community, and coordinate their services with those of related groups.

**Nurses and people**

- The nurse's primary responsibility is to those people who require nursing care.
- The nurse, in providing care, respects the beliefs, values, and customs of the individual.
- The nurse holds in confidence personal information and uses judgment in sharing this information.

**Nurses and practice**

- The nurse carries personal responsibility for nursing practice and for maintaining competence by continual learning.
- The nurse maintains the highest standards of nursing care possible within the reality of a specific situation.
- The nurse uses judgment in relation to individual competence when accepting and delegating responsibilities.
- The nurse, when acting in a professional capacity, should at all times maintain standards of personal conduct that would reflect credit upon the profession.

**Nurses and society**

- The nurse shares with other citizens the responsibility for initiating and supporting action to meet the health and social needs of the public.

**Nurses and coworkers**

- The nurse sustains a cooperative relationship with co-workers in nursing and other fields.
- The nurse takes appropriate action to safeguard the individual when his care is endangered by a coworker or any other person.

**Nurses and the profession**

- The nurse plays the major role in determining and implementing desirable standards of nursing practice and nursing education.
- The nurse is active in developing a core of professional knowledge.
- The nurse, acting through the professional organization, participates in establishing and maintaining equitable social and economic working conditions in nursing.

**F. The International Council of Nurses (ICN) Code of Ethics for Nurses**
1. General information
   a. The ICN Code of Ethics for Nurses was established in 1973 and reaffirmed in 1987 (see *International Council of Nurses Code of Ethics for Nurses,* page 23)
   b. The code is divided into two major sections: general nursing responsibilities and specific concerns of the profession
   c. The code emphasizes the nurse's obligations to the patient rather than to the physician, a departure from earlier thinking
2. Key ideas
   a. Nursing standards
   b. Health promotion and restoration
   c. Delivery of health services
   d. Professional accountability

**G. American Hospital Association (AHA) Patient's Bill of Rights**
1. General information
   a. The patient's rights must be considered when attempting to resolve ethical dilemmas in nursing
   b. The spirit of paternalism that dominated health care until the early 1970s severely limited a patient's rights to care
   c. A growing consumer movement gave more attention to patients' rights and the concept of the patient as a consumer of health care
   d. The patient's bill of rights was established in 1972 by the AHA to delineate the general rights of all patients (see *American Hospital Association Patient's Bill of Rights*)
   e. The patient's bill of rights outlines the rights of the hospitalized patient
   f. This bill of rights has no mechanism of enforcement for hospitals that choose not to follow it
   g. This bill of rights does not proclaim that all patients have an absolute right to health care
2. Key ideas
   a. Patient participation in decision making
   b. Privacy
   c. Confidentiality
   d. Informed consent
   e. Complete disclosure of information
   f. Refusal of treatment
   g. Continuity of care

**H. Making ethical decisions in nursing practice**
1. Most of the ethical dilemmas that nurses encounter do not have clear-cut solutions
2. Collaborative decision making to resolve complex ethical questions helps protect the professional from making unwise or erroneous decisions

# AMERICAN HOSPITAL ASSOCIATION PATIENT'S BILL OF RIGHTS

This policy document presents the official position of the American Hospital Association (AHA) as approved by the Board of Trustees and House of Delegates. During the 1970s the AHA Board of Trustees had a Committee on Health Care for the Disadvantaged, which developed the *Statement on a Patient's Bill of Rights*. That document was approved by the AHA House of Delegates on February 6, 1973, and has been published in various forms. This reprinting and reclassification conforms with the current classification system for AHA documents. The contents are unchanged.

The AHA presents a Patient's Bill of Rights with the expectation that observance of these rights will contribute to more effective patient care and greater satisfaction for the patient, his physician, and the hospital organization. Further, the Association presents these rights in the expectation that they will be supported by the hospital on behalf of its patients, as an integral part of the healing process. It is recognized that a personal relationship between the physician and the patient is essential for the provision of proper medical care. The traditional physician-patient relationship takes on a new dimension when care is rendered within an organizational structure. Legal precedent has established that the institution itself also has a responsibility to the patient. It is in recognition of these factors that these rights are affirmed.

1. The patient has the right to considerate and respectful care.

2. The patient has the right to obtain from his physician complete current information concerning his diagnosis, treatment, and prognosis in terms the patient can be reasonably expected to understand. When it is not medically advisable to give such information to the patient, the information should be made available to an appropriate person in his behalf. He has the right to know, by name, the physician responsible for coordinating his care.

3. The patient has the right to receive from his physician information necessary to give informed consent prior to the start of any procedure and/or treatment. Except in emergencies, such information for informed consent should include but not necessarily be limited to the specific procedure and/or treatment, the medically significant risks involved, and the probable duration of incapacitation. Where medically significant alternatives for care or treatment exist, or when the patient requests information concerning medical alternatives, the patient has the right to such information. The patient also has the right to know the name of the person responsible for the procedures and/or treatment.

4. The patient has the right to refuse treatment to the extent permitted by law and to be informed of the medical consequences of his action.

5. The patient has the right to every consideration of his privacy concerning his own medical care program. Case discussion, consultation, examination, and treatment are confidential and should be conducted discreetly. Those not directly involved in his care must have the permission of the patient to be present.

6. The patient has the right to expect that all communications and records pertaining to his care should be treated as confidential.

7. The patient has the right to expect that within its capacity a hospital must make reasonable response to the request of a patient for services. The hospital must provide evaluation, service, and/or referral as indicated by the urgency of the case.

continued

## AMERICAN HOSPITAL ASSOCIATION PATIENT'S BILL OF RIGHTS
continued

When medically permissible, a patient may be transferred to another facility only after he has received complete information and explanation concerning the needs for and alternatives to such a transfer. The institution to which the patient is to be transferred must first have accepted the patient for transfer.

8. The patient has the right to obtain information as to any relationship of his hospital to other health care and educational institutions insofar as his care is concerned. The patient has the right to obtain information as to the existence of any professional relationships among individuals, by name, who are treating him.

9. The patient has the right to be advised if the hospital proposes to engage in or perform human experimentation affecting his care or treatment. The patient has the right to refuse to participate in such research projects.

10. The patient has the right to expect reasonable continuity of care. He has the right to know in advance what appointment times and physicians are available and where. The patient has the right to expect that the hospital will provide a mechanism whereby he is informed by his physician or a delegate of the physician of the patient's continuing health care requirements following discharge.

11. The patient has the right to examine and receive an explanation of his bill regardless of source of payment.

12. The patient has the right to know what hospital rules and regulations apply to his conduct as a patient.

No catalog of rights can guarantee for the patient the kind of treatment he has a right to expect. A hospital has many functions to perform, including the prevention and treatment of disease, the education of both health professionals and patients, and the conduct of clinical research. All these activities must be conducted with an overriding concern for the patient, and, above all, the recognition of his dignity as a human being. Success in achieving this recognition assures success in the defense of the rights of the patient.

3. In all ethical dilemmas, the nurse should attempt to understand fully the moral issues involved
4. The nurse must follow several necessary steps in order to make an ethical decision
   a. Identify the dilemma as clearly as possible, using all available data
   b. Examine personal values as thoroughly as possible
   c. Identify the ethical principles involved in the dilemma
   d. Examine all possible solutions to the dilemma, regardless of the ethical principles involved
   e. Evaluate the likely outcome of each solution
   f. Choose the solution whose outcome is most in accord with personal values and ethical principles

## Points to Remember

Many sociocultural factors, including scientific and technological advances, influence ethical decision making.

Autonomy, justice, fidelity, and beneficence are the four basic concepts involved in ethical decision making; ethical codes are based in part on these four concepts.

The ANA Ethical Code for Nurses focuses on protecting the patient's rights while honoring obligations to the nursing profession and the public.

The AHA's Patient's Bill of Rights outlines the rights of a hospitalized patient.

## Glossary

**Collaborative decision making** — process of resolving dilemmas in consultation with other health care professionals to arrive at objective decisions

**Continuity of care** — health care that is centrally focused on the patient and coordinated among various members of the health care team, beginning with the patient's entrance into the health care system and continuing until discharge

**Patient advocate** — one (typically a nurse) who seeks to protect a patient's rights from infringement by institutional policies

# Ethical Issues in Nursing

**Learning Objectives**

After studying this section, the reader should be able to:

- Identify the important ethical issues that affect nursing today.

- Discuss significant ethical concerns involved in each issue.

- Describe ethical resolutions to the dilemmas posed by each issue.

## IV. Ethical Issues in Nursing

### A. Introduction

1. Like any profession, nursing is expected to maintain high ethical standards
2. Nursing's boundaries are marked by the ethical system nursing uses when providing care
   a. The ethical system helps the nurse make decisions about what is acceptable and unacceptable in nursing practice
   b. Although nursing's ethical system is based on time-tested principles, it must be dynamic to meet society's changing needs
3. The nurse and the patient may have different ethical systems
4. Many current ethical issues were not a concern 10 to 15 years ago
5. Rapid advances in technology and science, particularly in biology and medicine, have given rise to ethical dilemmas in health care
6. These dilemmas usually involve critical points in a person's existence, such as birth and death
7. Many of these dilemmas have no clear-cut solutions
8. Nurses have been challenged to think about the issues, to clarify their own values and ethical systems, and to make the best possible choices about how to resolve ethical dilemmas
9. Most ethical issues are further complicated by the legal questions they raise

### B. Informed consent

1. General information
   a. *Informed consent* is the permission obtained from a patient to have a test or procedure performed after the patient has been fully informed about the test or procedure; the consent may or may not be in writing, but a written consent provides better legal protection for health care workers
   b. Informed consent is based on the patient's right of *self-determination*
   c. Information given to the patient must include an explanation of the test or procedure, its potential risks and benefits, and any reasonable alternatives
   d. The patient must demonstrate that he understands the information; for instance, a nod of the head would be sufficient for a simple procedure, such as taking a patient's temperature, whereas a patient about to undergo surgery or a complicated diagnostic procedure should explain his understanding and sign a written consent form
   e. The patient must give the consent voluntarily, without coercion or persuasion
   f. The consent must be obtained by a physician before performing an invasive procedure or a procedure with considerable risks; a patient consents to routine aspects of care by signing a form on admission to the hospital

    g. The consent must be obtained before any preoperative medications or sedatives are administered to ensure that the patient's judgment is not impaired

    h. The patient must be mentally competent (having the mental and psychological capacity to make decisions)

    i. Competency in giving informed consent is a legal issue

2. Ethical concerns

    a. Spirit of *paternalism* still prevalent among some health care personnel

    b. Belief of some health care providers that the end justifies the means (any treatment or procedure is justified if the patient ultimately gets well)

    c. Overuse of *implied consent,* which should be used only in emergencies when an informed consent cannot be obtained

    d. Patient's fears of being disfavored by the health care team if he refuses to sign a consent form

    e. Competency of those who make decisions about invasive procedures

    f. Degree of understanding the patient must demonstrate for the informed consent to be valid

    g. Experimentation on patients with new medications, diagnostic tests, or surgical procedures

    h. Misunderstandings and confusion because of a patient's limited language skills or level of education

    i. Inability of health care personnel to predict all possible consequences of a test or procedure

    j. Patient's inability to remember explanations given just a few hours before the procedure

3. Ethical resolutions

    a. The key purpose of informed consent is to ensure the patient's right to self-determination in health care

    b. The *reasonable patient standard* provides a guideline for disclosing information

    c. The nurse should strive to gain the patient's confidence and trust when providing information, thereby contributing to maximum recovery

## C. Right to die

1. General information

    a. A patient's right to die involves the issue of whether to provide or withhold lifesaving measures

    b. People view death from different perspectives; some think of death as the ending of all vital functions, whereas others may define it as a life without dignity

    c. Most states recognize the American Medical Association's definition of *brain death,* developed in 1979, as the legal definition of death

    d. Extraordinary means of health care, sometimes called heroic measures, are life-sustaining therapies, treatments, equipment, or medications used to maintain and prolong a patient's life; these measures (including ventilators, intra-aortic balloon pumps, colostomies, cardiac defibrillation, tube-feeding, total parenteral nutrition, and pacemakers) can be costly, highly invasive, complicated, and potentially dangerous

    e. The right to die involves the concept of euthanasia, a term meaning "painless death"

    f. *Positive euthanasia* (also called active euthanasia or mercy killing) refers to situations in which life-support systems are withdrawn or a medication, treatment, or procedure is used to bring about death

    g. *Negative euthanasia* (also called passive euthanasia) refers to situations in which no extraordinary or heroic life-support measures are used to save a person's life

    h. A *living will* or *natural death statement* is a person's written request that no extraordinary procedures be used to sustain or prolong life; living wills are legally binding (see Appendix A, Living Will, for more information)

    i. A durable power of attorney, when executed, helps ensure that the instructions detailed in the living will are carried out (see Appendix B, Durable Power of Attorney, for more information)

2. Ethical concerns

    a. The health care system's orientation toward saving and prolonging lives and thus its opposition to withholding life-sustaining treatments

    b. *Do-not-resuscitate (DNR) orders,* also called *no code* situations, which are considered forms of passive euthanasia

    c. Decision-making conflicts over a patient's right to die

    d. Disagreements about what constitutes extraordinary means of health care

    e. Questions about whether the same ethical principles that apply to adult patients also apply to pediatric patients

    f. The nurse's role in the right-to-die issue

3. Ethical resolutions

    a. The health care team, the patient, and the family must mutually decide whether a prolonged but sometimes painful extension of life is worse than immediate death

    b. A living will is a legal document and must be upheld by the patient's family and all health care providers

    c. Nurses must resolve personal feelings about death and quality of life when caring for a terminally ill patient

## D. Substance abuse among nurses

1. General information

    a. A nurse who ingests, injects, or inhales a mind-altering substance cannot practice nursing safely and competently

    b. A practicing nurse will probably encounter a chemically impaired co-worker sometime during her career

    c. About 40,000 nurses who work in the United States are alcoholic

    d. Drug addiction among U.S. nurses is estimated to be 30 to 100 times greater than that among the general population; authorities are unable to determine a more precise estimate because thousands of nurses are treated or discharged without having their addiction made public

    e. Nurses have easy access to drugs because they usually are responsible for obtaining and maintaining the supply of controlled drugs on a hospital unit

    f. Factors contributing to increased substance abuse among nurses include job stress, rotating shifts, staff shortages, unrealistic expectations of the employer, frustration, anxiety, depression, and lack of autonomy in practice

    g. Nearly 70% of the disciplinary actions taken by state boards of nursing involve substance abuse

    h. Chemically impaired nurses usually exhibit characteristic behaviors (see *Profile of a Chemically Impaired Nurse*)

2. Ethical concerns

    a. Professional and emotional conflicts felt by the chemically impaired nurse's colleagues, who must use their training as promoters of health to try to understand the nurse's abuse of health

    b. Unsatisfactory response of supervisors, who sometimes protect, transfer, or promote the substance abuser rather than acknowledge the problem

## PROFILE OF A CHEMICALLY IMPAIRED NURSE

Substance abuse among nurses is not an uncommon problem. Chances are, each nurse will encounter a chemically impaired coworker at some time, and each nurse has a responsibility to report such a colleague. The following characteristics and situations typify the behavior of a nurse who is abusing a substance.

- Increased absenteeism
- Avoidance of new and challenging assignments
- Sudden mood swings and personality changes
- Incoherent or incomplete charting
- Increased errors in treatment, particularly in dosage computation
- Poor personal hygiene and appearance
- Inability to concentrate or remember details
- Alcohol on the breath and flushed face
- Slurred speech and unsteady gait
- Discrepancies in narcotic supplies detected at the end of the nurse's shift
- Narcotics signed out to patients only on the nurse's shift
- Patient complaints of no relief from narcotics supposedly administered when the nurse is on duty
- Preference for working alone or on the night shift, when supervision is minimal

    c. Violation of the patient's right to safe and effective care

    d. Increased work loads and stress on colleagues

    e. Conflicting loyalties over whether to report a colleague who is a substance abuser

3. Ethical resolutions

    a. A chemically impaired nurse is incompetent to practice nursing and must be removed from the patient care setting

    b. The nurse must be certain that a substance abuse problem exists by carefully collecting and documenting incidents, including specific dates and times, before reporting a chemically impaired nurse

    c. Confronting or accusing the suspected nurse directly is unwise

    d. The nurse files a report through the institution's usual chain of command, starting with the unit manager, then the supervisor, and finally the director of nursing

    e. If the institution's administration takes no action, the nurse should submit the report to the state board of nursing

    f. The report should be well-documented and signed, and it should include a request for confidentiality, if appropriate

## E. Abortion

1. General information

    a. *Abortion,* one of the oldest surgical procedures recorded in history, refers to the expulsion of a fetus from the uterus before 28 weeks' gestation

    b. Greek and Roman civilizations used abortion for practical purposes — to control population growth

    c. Early Jewish and Christian religions highly valued human life, even in the prebirth state, and hence forbade abortion on both religious and practical grounds

    d. *Spontaneous abortion* (also called miscarriage) occurs naturally from medical problems of the pregnant patient or the fetus

    e. *Induced abortion* (also called therapeutic abortion) occurs intentionally when a pregnancy is terminated by artificial methods

    f. The status of the fetus as a human life is an important element in the abortion controversy

    g. Bioethicists use measurable criteria of human body development (such as fetal movement and the existence of a heart and nervous system) to determine when the fetus is alive

    h. In *Roe v. Wade* (1973), the U.S. Supreme Court established that a person may act on private convictions about situations involving one's own body; the Court did not make a moral or ethical decision about what constitutes human life or whether abortion is morally permissible

2. Ethical concerns

    a. Disagreements about whether or not a fetus is a human being entitled to the same rights as other human beings

      b. Uncertainty about the point at which a fetus can live outside the mother's womb (currently 20 to 24 weeks, but new technology and life-support equipment may reduce this number further)

      c. Conflicts between a woman's rights, including the right to control her own body, and the rights of a fetus or the rights of the other parties in conception

  3. Ethical resolutions

      a. Nurses should examine their own views on abortion and periodically re-evaluate these views in light of new medical, scientific, or technological information

      b. If personal values do not allow participation in care of abortion patients, nurses should refuse positions in which such situations are likely to arise

## F. In vitro fertilization

  1. General information

      a. *In vitro fertilization* is the process of removing ova from a woman's uterus, placing them in a petri dish filled with a sterilized growth medium, and covering them with healthy motile spermatozoa for fertilization; three to five ova are re-implanted in the woman's uterus 10 to 14 days after fertilization, and the remaining fertilized ova are frozen for future use or discarded

      b. In vitro fertilization can use the husband's sperm (homologous) or a donor's sperm (heterologous) to fertilize the ova

      c. The first successful in vitro fertilization took place in 1978, although the first research in animals may have started as early as 1878

      d. Infertility is the most common reason for using in vitro fertilization; other reasons include family planning and sex predetermination

      e. In vitro fertilization is a necessary step in surrogate procreation (see "Surrogate motherhood" for more information)

  2. Ethical concerns

      a. Scientific manipulation of the ova and sperm, hailed by some people as an opportunity for couples to have children after other infertility treatments have failed but denounced by others as a circumvention of the natural order that has the potential to produce an abnormal infant

      b. Conflicting rights of the infertile couple, the fetus, the physician, other health care personnel, and society

      c. Uncertainty over parental responsibility — and the potential for incestuous conception or marriage — when the procedure uses donor sperm

      d. Potential abuses of in vitro fertilization, such as black market operations or attempts to create "superior races" through predetermination of sex by sperm type

      e. Uncertainty over the rights of an infant who could develop from fertilized ova that had been frozen and stored indefinitely — and uncertainty about who would raise the infant

    f.   Potential disregard of parental responsibility if an infant is born with congenital defects

    g.   Questions involving the rights, if any, of discarded fertilized ova

3.   Ethical resolutions

    a.   Nurses must examine their own position on the ethics of in vitro fertilization before working with a patient who is considering or has chosen the procedure

    b.   Nurses opposed to in vitro fertilization should not be involved in caring for a patient who opts for this procedure

    c.   All nurses should be aware of the potentials for abuse that this procedure holds

## G. Surrogate motherhood

1.   General information

    a.   A *surrogate mother* is a woman who gives birth after carrying the fertilized ovum of another woman or, more commonly, after being artificially inseminated with sperm from the biological father; in the latter case, the infant is then legally adopted by the wife of the biological father

    b.   More than 1,000 surrogate births have occurred since the first one, in England in 1976

    c.   Nearly 20% of American couples are infertile; in 60% to 70% of these cases, the female is infertile

    d.   Major reasons for couples to choose surrogate motherhood include the woman's inability to become pregnant or carry a fetus to term, the woman's age or other pregnancy-related health risks, and the shortage of infants available for adoption

    e.   Surrogate mother programs (such as Surrogate Parenting Associates, Inc., and Surrogate Family Services, Inc.) have been established to provide services to the surrogate mother and the infertile couple

    f.   A surrogate birth poses no greater risk of physical danger to the fetus or mother than does a normal birth

2.   Ethical concerns

    a.   Conflicting rights of the surrogate mother, the infertile couple, the fetus, and society

    b.   Inadequacy of existing laws to address the difficult legal and ethical questions raised by this issue

    c.   Possibility that surrogate mother contracts (which stipulate that the surrogate mother surrender the infant at birth) violate adoption laws (which prevent a mother from surrendering parental rights before the infant is born)

    d.   Advertising of services by potential surrogate mothers, with fees ranging from $50,000 to $150,000 per infant, leading many people to view surrogate motherhood as infant selling

    e.   Difficulty in determining the legal father if the surrogate mother has a spouse or partner

      f. Uncertainty over responsibility for the infant's care if neither the infertile couple nor the surrogate mother wants the infant (for instance, if the infant is born with a handicap) or if the surrogate mother refuses to surrender the infant after giving birth

      g. Potential exploitation of infertile couples whose desire to have an infant leaves them vulnerable to financial and emotional blackmail

  3. Ethical resolutions

      a. Federal and state laws, uniformly worded and based on sound ethical principles, are needed to deal with the various concerns arising from surrogate motherhood

      b. Nurses should examine their personal views on surrogate motherhood—and become familiar with the legal and ethical pitfalls it presents—before working with surrogate mothers or infertile couples who decide to contract with a surrogate

## H. Organ transplantation

  1. General information

      a. Organ transplantation, a generally accepted and widely practiced medical procedure, is the removal of organs or tissues from one person for implantation in another person

      b. Organs and tissues that have been transplanted include the kidney, heart, lungs, liver, pancreatic tissue, bone tissue, cornea, blood, bone marrow, and skin

      c. The main criteria for organ donor recipients are medical need, organ match, and availability and location of donor

      d. An *autograft* is the removal of tissue from one part of the body to be used on another part of the same body

      e. A *homograft* is the transplantation of organs or tissues from one individual to another of the same species

      f. A *living related donor* involves a homograft to be used on a relative, usually an identical twin or a sibling

      g. A *cadaver donor* involves a homograft from a deceased person, usually not a relative

      h. New immunosuppressant agents have led to dramatic increases in survival rates for organ transplant recipients

      i. Transplant technology, although fairly well developed, continues to advance with the development of new procedures, immunosuppressant agents, and methods to preserve harvested organs

  2. Ethical concerns

      a. Conflicting rights of the donor, the recipient, their families, and society

      b. Potential for elitism when choosing one recipient over another

      c The tremendous expense of organ transplantation, uncertainty over who should pay the expense (many insurance companies will not), and disagreements about whether the money should be used instead to benefit larger numbers of people, such as to fund acquired immunodeficiency syndrome research or housing for the homeless

      d. Potential abuse of informed consent, especially in cases involving children or mentally handicapped persons

      e. Difficulty in determining exactly when an organ can be removed (organs should be removed immediately after death, but not all states define death in the same way)

      f. The length of time an irreversibly comatose patient should remain on life-support equipment solely to provide a healthy organ for transplantation

      g. Acceptance of a flat electroencephalogram as evidence of death, even though the heart and other autonomic systems may be functioning with or without life-support equipment

      h. The family's rights to the body versus those of the state when cadaver organs are used

      i. Violation of the traditional respect for the body when organs are removed after death

  3. Ethical resolutions

      a. Issues of informed consent are usually resolved under the Uniform Anatomical Gift Act, which allows people to donate their organs in a will, in an agreement on a driver's license, or in some other written form (see Appendix C, Uniform Anatomical Gift Act, for more information)

      b. Removing an organ from a child or a mentally incompetent adult for the purpose of transplantation is never ethical

      c. Most states and medical facilities view the use of aborted fetal tissue for transplantation as unethical and usually illegal

      d. Nurses have a moral and (in some states) legal obligation to identify potential organ donors and to notify the organization responsible for coordinating transplant activities

      e. Nurses who work in critical care or emergency departments should re-examine their commitment to organ donation so they can feel comfortable when asking families about transplantation and providing emotional support to the families during this time of sadness and loss

## I. Right to treatment

  1. General information

      a. A *right* is a claim or privilege to which one is justly entitled

      b. Rights involve a society's legal and ethical systems and include *realized rights* (recognized by society and protected by law, such as the right to privacy), *unrealized rights* (neither recognized by society nor protected by law, such as the right to health care), *general rights* (arising out of the principle of equity in the relationship between an individual and society or large institutions, such as hospitals), and *special rights* (developing between two individuals in a particular transaction or relationship, such as between a nurse and a patient)

      c. General rights usually supercede special rights

      d. Individual rights evolve from society's perception of "rights"

   e.  The concept of individual rights probably resulted from society's fear of
       and dependence on social and economic systems and on organizations
       that tended to overlook the individual
   f.  Legal rights come from the state and are ordered by law; a legal right
       refers to a person's power to change something or keep it the same
   g.  Although a person may assert a given right, the right is not always legal
   h.  The right to health is, at best, a tentative and unenforceable right with
       no legal foundation, although virtually everyone agrees that an ill person
       who enters the health care system has a right to receive treatment
       appropriate to the illness
   i.  The right to treatment was not always perceived so universally, as when
       psychiatric patients were kept in institutions just to keep them off the
       streets
2. Ethical concerns
   a.  Lack of equal access to health care for all individuals because of the
       inability of some to pay for it
   b.  Potential conflict between the obligation of health care professionals to
       provide a patient with the best possible care and the patient's right to
       self-determination
   c.  A child's right to treatment versus the parents' right to refuse treatment
       (usually for religious reasons)
3. Ethical resolutions
   a.  Nurses must be guided by the principle that health care should be
       available to all individuals, regardless of ability to pay for the care
   b.  The American Nurses' Association Code of Ethics requires nurses to
       provide care for patients regardless of religion, sex, or race
   c.  If a nurse's position on the right-to-treatment issue threatens to interfere
       with the treatments a patient receives or refuses, the nurse should ask to
       be reassigned to a different patient

## J.  Behavior control in health care
1. General information
   a.  Throughout history, people have tried to understand, predict, influence,
       and control human behavior
   b.  Every society has behavioral conventions, rules, and norms to which all
       members are expected to conform
   c.  The preservation of a civilized society largely depends on the
       government's ability to enforce its rules and norms among its citizens
   d.  Society determines whether behavior is normal or abnormal, acceptable
       or unacceptable
   e.  Society tolerates certain types of nonconformists (such as communal
       living groups and nudists) whose life-styles, beliefs, and behavior do not
       differ substantially from acceptable norms

f. Unacceptable, abnormal, or deviant behavior is a thought or action that conflicts with the thoughts or actions of the majority and that society cannot understand or condone

g. Deviance is not an inherent quality of a thought or act but a result of the application of social rules and norms to the thought or act

h. Abnormal groups in society (such as mentally ill or mentally retarded persons, substance abusers, and criminals) cannot always be identified by physical appearance

i. The term *dangerous,* referring to the likelihood that an individual will cause physical harm to himself or others, is commonly used as a criterion to commit the individual to a mental institution or prison

j. Predicting how dangerous a person is to himself or others is usually difficult because of the lack of clear criteria

k. *Behavior control* refers to a wide range of activities or treatments imposed on or offered to an individual, either to make that individual conform to the wishes of another person or society or to control abnormal, deviant, or dangerous behavior

l. Common methods of behavior control include psychotherapy, aversive therapy, desensitization, psychopharmacology, electroconvulsive therapy, psychosurgery, and rehabilitation techniques

m. The ultimate goal of behavior control is to make a person behave in a way that satisfies the expectations of society

2. Ethical concerns

a. Conflict between the individual's right to freedom (including the right to self-determination and the right to refuse treatment) and society's obligation to maintain the social order

b. Misuse of behavior control to suppress personal freedom unjustifiably

c. Deprivation of a mentally ill patient's right to choose his course of treatment without coercion

d. Behavioral changes that satisfy the community or society but do not meet and perhaps contradict the patient's wishes and needs

e. Conflicts of interest that can occur in mental institutions and prisons, where staff members serve double roles as therapeutic agents for the patient or inmate and as controlling agents for the state

f. Uncertainty over the amount and types of coercion that are ethical to use

g. Potential for conflict if a therapist attempts to satisfy personal interests at the expense of a patient's needs (for instance, a therapist who has a personal interest in electroconvulsive therapy may order such treatments for a patient whose condition does not warrant them)

h. Undue pressure exerted on the therapist by a third party (such as a family member, the therapist's supervisor, or a hospital administrator) to keep the patient institutionalized

i. The degree to which an individual's right to personal integrity and identity is an inviolable, absolute right, particularly in cases that involve deviancy or possible danger to the individual or to others

j. Society's obligation to protect all of its members, even those considered deviant or dangerous

     k.   Paternalism and authoritarianism toward mentally ill patients because of their limited capacity to make decisions

     l.   Inability to obtain informed consent from those declared mentally ill

3.   Ethical resolutions

     a.   Health care workers should follow basic guidelines to preserve a patient's freedom during behavior control (see *Kittrie Therapeutic Bill of Rights*)

     b.   Because a nurse has the power to influence a patient's course of treatment, with or without the patient's permission, psychiatric nurses should make an extra effort to involve the patient in the plan of care to prevent coercion and infringement of the patient's rights

     c.   Nurses should treat any communication from a mentally ill patient with the same seriousness they give to other patients

     d.   Nurses must not allow the patient to be reduced to the status of a child nor allow the health care team to violate the patient's right to participate in decision making about his care

## KITTRIE THERAPEUTIC BILL OF RIGHTS

Formulated in 1971, the Kittrie Therapeutic Bill of Rights combines humansim and utilitarianism in its approach to the care of patients with mental illness. The Mental Health Patient's Bill of Rights (Public law 96-398-U.S.C. Sec. 9501) subsequently adopted many of the principles and concepts outlined here.

• No person shall be compelled to undergo treatment except for the defense of society.

• A person's innate right to remain free of excessive forms of human modification (such as psychosurgery) shall be inviolable.

• No social sanctions may be invoked by a health care institution unless the person subjected to treatment has demonstrated a clear and present danger through harmful behavior that has already occurred or is immediately forthcoming.

• No person shall be subjected to involuntary incarceration or treatment solely because a mental disorder has been diagnosed, nor shall the conviction for a crime or a finding of "not guilty by reason of insanity" suffice to have a person automatically committed or treated.

• No social sanctions—whether criminal, civil, or therapeutic—may be invoked by the legal system unless the patient has a judicial or other independent hearing, appointed counsel, and an opportunity to confront those testifying about his past conduct or therapeutic needs.

• Dual interference by the legal and medical communities is prohibited (thus, a patient being treated for a mental illness cannot be simultaneously punished by the courts).

• An involuntary patient shall have the right to refuse treatment.

• Any compulsory treatment must be the least required reasonably to protect society.

• All committed persons should have direct access to appointed counsel and the right, without interference, to petition the courts for relief (the right to refuse treatment and be released from the institution).

• Those submitting to voluntary treatment should not be subsequently transferred to a compulsory program through administrative action.

From Kittrie, N.N. *The Right to be Different.* Baltimore: John Hopkins University Press, 1971. Adapted with permission of the publisher.

  e.  Nurses must avoid abusing behavior-control techniques in dealing with
      all patients
  f.  Nurses should favor noninvasive behavior-control methods that maintain
      the patient's self-respect, dignity, and identity; such methods do not rely
      on coercion, fear, or deception nor do they decrease his ability to think
      rationally
  g.  Nurses must remember that a patient has the right to refuse any form of
      behavior-control treatment

## K.  Eugenics and genetic manipulation
  1.  General information
      a.  Scientific understanding and knowledge of gene structure has advanced
          tremendously in recent years
      b.  Each cell of an organism carries a genetic blueprint for the entire
          organism
      c.  Scientists have identified certain chromosomes on genes and can control
          certain attributes or functions of the cell and organism through genetic
          manipulation
      d.  Present genetic manipulation includes production of biologics (such as
          antibiotics) and hormones (such as insulin) by altering bacteria and has
          increased understanding of cancer cells and how to control them
      e.  Future uses may include genetic manipulation of the gene pool to
          produce superior individuals and new pathogenic species
      f.  Eugenics (the science of improving a species through control of the
          hereditary factors by manipulation of the gene pool) is commonly used
          to improve livestock and crop production and has many moral and
          ethical concerns for use in humans
      g.  Other genetic manipulation techniques include cloning, *somatic
          alteration, germ cell alteration,* and *recombinant DNA synthesis*
  2.  Ethical concerns
      a.  An individual's basic right to know (and thus a scientist's right to seek
          knowledge and conduct research) versus the public's right to protection
          and safety
      b.  Beneficial consequences of new knowledge and discovery versus
          potentially harmful consequences
      c.  Potential for creating a new pathogenic species that cannot be controlled
          through genetic manipulation
  3.  Ethical resolutions
      a.  Each scientific discovery and decision should be considered in light of its
          moral and ethical value and its cost and benefit to the public
      b.  Scientific research, especially that of genetic manipulation, needs
          technological and moral safeguards
      c.  Nurses should support laws that regulate genetic manipulation
      d.  Nurses involved in genetic research must be mindful of its potential
          problems and direct their research to benefit society

## Points to Remember

Most health care issues that present ethical dilemmas for nurses have arisen from rapid advances in science and technology.

These dilemmas usually involve a conflict of rights, either between individuals or between individuals and society.

Rarely does one person or group have an absolute right over another person or group.

Resolution of ethical dilemmas requires one to make rational decisions after careful consideration of all available information.

## Glossary

**Artificial insemination** — introduction of semen into the vagina or cervix, using instruments, syringes, or other technology

**Brain death** — irreversible cessation of brain functioning accompanied by ongoing biological functioning in all other parts of the human body, the latter maintained with ventilators, vasopressor drugs, and other life-support measures

**Deviance** — behavior that is different from the generally accepted "normal" behavior of a group or society

**Germ cell alteration** — changes in the structure of DNA during the earliest stages of cell growth

**Health care paternalism** — belief that procedures are performed in the patient's best interest and that the patient need not be given complete information or options

**Implied consent** — patient's presumed agreement to a medical procedure or test, usually in a life-threatening emergency when the patient cannot grant an informed consent

**In vitro fertilization** — process of fertilization outside the body by removing a number of ova, placing them in a petri dish filled with a sterilized growth medium, and covering them with healthy spermatozoa

**Reasonable patient standard** — amount of information that a reasonable patient needs to know about a test or procedure before granting informed consent

## **Glossary** continued

**Recombinant DNA synthesis** — process of inserting segments of DNA from one species into the DNA of another species

**Self-determination** — individual's right to decide how and where to live without interference from others

**Somatic alteration** — in vitro isolation of a specific gene that is then synthetically reproduced in the laboratory

# Overview of Law in Society and Health Care

**Learning Objectives**

After studying this section, the reader should be able to:

● Define natural law.

● Describe the legal system as it applies to nursing.

● Describe the three major sources of law: statutory, administrative, and common law.

● Explain the four basic principles on which all law is based: concern for justice and fairness, need for laws to be pliable, application of similar standards of performance, and individual rights and responsibilities.

● Describe the judicial system, including court jurisdiction and the state and federal court tier systems.

● List the steps in the trial process.

● Identify the significance of statutes of limitation and expert witnesses.

## V. Overview of Law in Society and Health Care

**A. Introduction**
1. *Laws* are the body of rules, guidelines, and regulations that govern society and protect the health, safety, and welfare of its citizens
   a. All law is ultimately derived from *natural law*—the innate human tendency to do good and avoid evil
   b. Throughout history, different societies have developed similar fundamental rules or laws based on natural law
2. The U.S federal government and the states hold constitutional authority to create and enforce laws
   a. The legal system sets guidelines rather than rigid rules for practice
   b. All laws, regardless of origin, are subject to change and interpretation
   c. Laws and court decisions are recorded as citations in references such as legal encyclopedias and legal texts; these citations are often used in the legal process (see Appendix E, Interpreting Legal Citations, for more information)
3. The government and the legal system are outgrowths of the need to manage complex human interactions; the larger, more complex, and less homogeneous the group is, the more complex and detailed the rules must be
4. Society has become extraordinarily complex and so have its various institutions, such as the health care system
   a. Increased interaction between the health care system and the law results directly from health care's increased complexity, size, and ability to save and prolong human life
   b. Federal and state laws and the self-imposed regulations of the nursing profession directly shape and influence nursing practice
   c. The first mandatory nurse practice act, passed in 1938 in New York, marked the integration of law with nursing
5. The legal system continues to exert considerable influence on nursing
   a. Many nurses are overwhelmed by the law and the legal restrictions placed on the health care system
   b. All nurses should try to understand the concepts and mechanisms of law and must respect the legal restrictions on health care
   c. Nurses' preoccupation with the threat of lawsuits is sometimes self-generated and unwarranted
   d. A basic knowledge of the law and how it works can help nurses avoid litigation and allow them to practice nursing confidently
   e. The threat of legal consequences, although troublesome to some nurses, has nevertheless improved the quality of patient care, highlighted the need for professional accountability, and led to the establishment of the evaluation process in the health care disciplines

**B. Sources of law**
1. General information
   a. Laws are established and enforced by legislative authority (such as a judge or governmental agency) to regulate human social conduct in a formally prescribed and legally binding manner

      b. If humans did not interact, no laws would be needed
      c. Laws are derived from one of three sources: statutory law, administrative law, or common law
  2. Statutory law
      a. *Statutory law* is established and enforced by federal or state legislators in response to perceived needs for social regulation
      b. Statutory laws help maintain a government's right to uphold the social order and to protect the rights of individuals
      c. The nurse practice acts of the 50 states and of the District of Columbia are examples of statutory laws
  3. Administrative law
      a. *Administrative law* is established by legislators but enforced by an administrative agency on the authority of the legislators
      b. Administrative agencies are run by individuals whose expertise in a given field empowers them to enforce administrative laws governing that field
      c. These agencies also have the authority to create rules and regulations that take on the force of statutory laws but that are enforceable only to the limits granted by the legislators
      d. State boards of nursing and medical boards are examples of administrative agencies
  4. Common law
      a. *Common law* (also called judicial or decisional law) is established by judicial decisions to resolve legal disputes
      b. In deciding cases, the courts either interpret a statute or regulation or decide which of two conflicting statutes or regulations applies in a given situation
      c. According to the principle of precedent in common law, cases with fact patterns similar to those of cases previously decided by the court should result in similar decisions
      d. Precedent is not absolute; a different decision can be rendered by a court in a jurisdiction outside that of the initial trial, or a court can make a landmark decision, which departs from precedent because of changes in societal needs or technology

## C. Principles of law
  1. General information
      a. Four basic principles serve as underpinnings for the entire legal system: a concern for justice and fairness, a need for laws to be pliable, application of similar standards of performance, and individual rights and responsibilities
      b. Although legal issues and court cases can become complex, most of their underlying arguments are based on one of these four principles
  2. Concern for justice and fairness
      a. The legal system is based on a concern for justice and fairness in protecting the rights of one individual or group from infringement by the actions of other individuals or groups

    b. This principle is a method of managing the complex social actions within society in an orderly manner

3. Need for laws to be pliable
    a. As changes occur in a social structure, the society's legal system also must change
    b. Because social and technological changes occur more rapidly than legal changes, the legal system usually is in the position of reacting to new situations
    c. Laws should be dynamic to accommodate new legal issues that arise with technological advancement

4. Similar standards of performance
    a. Although all individuals are not held to the same standards, those with similar education, experience, and background are expected to act in a similar manner
    b. In this context, a person's actions are judged by universally accepted standards of what a prudent and reasonable person with similar training would do in similar circumstances

5. Individual rights and responsibilities
    a. Each person possesses inherent rights and corresponding responsibilities
    b. The more rights a person claims, the greater his responsibilities
    c. Failure to meet responsibilities can lead to limitation of rights

**D. Judicial system**
1. General information
    a. The judicial system attempts to resolve legal controversies over questions of fact, law, or both (for instance, a negligence lawsuit against a nurse may involve a question of fact, whereas a patient's request to terminate life support may involve a question of law)
    b. In any legal controversy, facts are determined by examining evidence presented by lawyers for each side of the controversy
    c. Facts are sometimes difficult to determine because different people may perceive the same incident in different ways
    d. In factual disputes, a jury is responsible for determining what actually happened, based on the evidence presented, and rendering a verdict
    e. In a legal controversy in which both sides agree on the facts, the question to be resolved is one of application and interpretation of the law; in such cases, the judge or magistrate makes the decision rather than a jury
    f. The judicial process in the United States is based on court jurisdiction and consists of state and federal court tiers

2. Court jurisdiction
    a. *Court jurisdiction* refers to a court's authority to hear a case and determine judicial action in a given place at a given time

    b. Jurisdiction is determined by several factors, including class of case and location of the transgression or dispute

    c. *Subject matter jurisdiction* refers to a court's authority to hear and decide a case within a particular class of cases, such as the authority of probate courts

## TIER SYSTEM OF STATE AND FEDERAL COURTS

| COURT LEVEL | OTHER NAMES USED | PRIMARY FUNCTIONS |
|---|---|---|
| **State Court Tier System** | | |
| Trial court | • Original court of jurisdiction<br>• Circuit court<br>• Court of common pleas<br>• District court<br>• Chancery court<br>• Superior court | • Determines applicable law<br>• Presents and evaluates law facts<br>• Renders decision of judge or jury |
| Intermediate court of appeals | • Intermediate appellate courts<br>• Appellate division of supreme court<br>• Superior court<br>• Court of special appeals<br>• Court of civil or criminal appeals | • Bases decision about appeal on evidence presented in trial record |
| Final court of appeal | • State court of last resort<br>• Supreme judicial court<br>• Court of appeal | • Hears appeals from intermediate court<br>• Adopts rules of procedure for state<br>• Licenses attorneys in that state<br>• Interprets state statutes and constitution |
| **Federal Court Tier System** | | |
| Original trial court | • U.S. district court<br>• Specialty court (such as court of claims, bankruptcy court, and patent court) | • Tries cases involving federal law or interstate residents |
| Intermediate federal court of appeals | • U.S. circuit court<br>• U.S. court of appeals | • Hears appeals from trial courts in 12 U.S. districts |
| Final federal court of appeals | • U.S. Supreme Court | • Hears appeals from federal courts of appeal or state supreme courts in matters of federal law or constitution |

    d. *Personal jurisdiction* refers to a court's authority to render judgments against an individual in a particular location at a particular time; determined in part by the type of legal transgression committed, personal jurisdiction usually emanates from the court of the county in which the individual resides

    e. *Concurrent jurisdiction* exists when more than one court is qualified to hear a case, such as one involving many defendants from different states

    f. The defendant's lawyer usually chooses the court jurisdiction most favorable to the defendant

3. State court system

    a. The state court system consists of three tiers, with cases beginning at the lowest level (trial courts) and progressing to higher levels (intermediate and final courts of appeal)

    b. The final court of appeal usually is called the State Supreme Court

    c. Either the plaintiff or the defendant can appeal an unfavorable decision from a lower court to a higher court

    d. The state court system can be confusing to the uninitiated because the courts are known by various names in different regions of the country

4. Federal court system

    a. The federal court system also consists of three tiers (the original federal trial courts, intermediate federal courts, and a final federal court)

    b. The final court of appeal in the United States is the U.S. Supreme Court

    c. Either the plaintiff or the defendant can appeal an unfavorable decision from a lower court to a higher court (see *Tier System of State and Federal Courts*)

**E. Trial process**

1. General information

    a. The *trial process* is a systematic method of legal decision making that begins with the initiation of a complaint and ends with a final judgment (see *Trial Process: Step by Step,* pages 50 and 51)

    b. The trial process always involves a plaintiff and a defendant

    c. The trial process is somewhat limited by several factors, including the statute of limitations, which restricts the time during which a plaintiff can file a lawsuit to redress an injury or illegal act

    d. Expert witnesses may be called to appear in a trial to explain technical information or offer opinions based on their specialized knowledge and expertise

2. Basic steps of the trial process

    a. A lawsuit is initiated when a plaintiff contacts a lawyer to determine if a valid complaint exists against a defendant

    b. *Pleading* and *pretrial motions* are documents that set forth the facts as perceived by the defendant and the plaintiff; these documents serve as the basis for the legal claims of both parties

(Text continues on page 52.)

## TRIAL PROCESS: STEP BY STEP

Being named as a defendant in a lawsuit can be confusing as well as stressful. The antidote is knowing what to expect. This chart summarizes the basic trial process from complaint to execution of judgment.

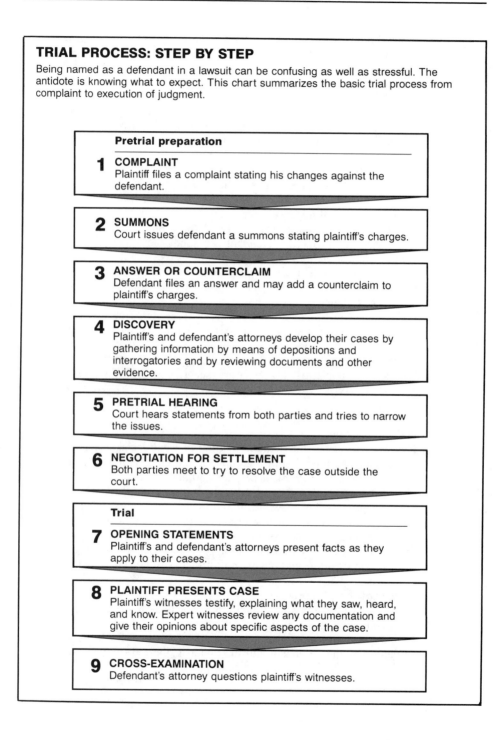

**Pretrial preparation**

**1 COMPLAINT**
Plaintiff files a complaint stating his changes against the defendant.

**2 SUMMONS**
Court issues defendant a summons stating plaintiff's charges.

**3 ANSWER OR COUNTERCLAIM**
Defendant files an answer and may add a counterclaim to plaintiff's charges.

**4 DISCOVERY**
Plaintiff's and defendant's attorneys develop their cases by gathering information by means of depositions and interrogatories and by reviewing documents and other evidence.

**5 PRETRIAL HEARING**
Court hears statements from both parties and tries to narrow the issues.

**6 NEGOTIATION FOR SETTLEMENT**
Both parties meet to try to resolve the case outside the court.

**Trial**

**7 OPENING STATEMENTS**
Plaintiff's and defendant's attorneys present facts as they apply to their cases.

**8 PLAINTIFF PRESENTS CASE**
Plaintiff's witnesses testify, explaining what they saw, heard, and know. Expert witnesses review any documentation and give their opinions about specific aspects of the case.

**9 CROSS-EXAMINATION**
Defendant's attorney questions plaintiff's witnesses.

**TRIAL PROCESS: STEP BY STEP** continued

**10 PLAINTIFF CLOSES CASE**
Defendant's attorney may make a motion to dismiss the case, claiming plaintiff's evidence is insufficient.

**11 DEFENDANT PRESENTS CASE**
Defendant's witnesses testify, explaining what they saw, heard, and know. Expert witnesses review any documentation and give their opinions about specific aspects of the case.

**12 CROSS-EXAMINATION**
Plaintiff's attorney questions defendant's witnesses.

**13 DEFENDANT CLOSES CASE**
Plaintiff's attorney may claim defendant hasn't presented an issue for the jury to decide.

**14 CLOSING STATEMENTS**
Each attorney summarizes his case for the jury.

**15 JURY INSTRUCTION**
Judge instructs the jury in points of law that apply in this particular case.

**16 JURY DELIBERATION**
Jury reviews facts and votes on verdict.

**17 VERDICT**
Jury announces verdict before judge and both parties.

**18 APPEAL (optional)**
Attorneys review transcripts. The party against whom the court rule may appeal if he feels the judge didn't interpret the law properly, instruct the jury properly, or conduct the trial properly.

**19 EXECUTION OF JUDGMENT**
Appeals process is completed and the case is settled.

     c. *Pretrial procurement of evidence,* or *discovery,* allows the plaintiff and the defendant to question witnesses, seek depositions, and collect evidence to be used during the trial

     d. The *trial* is the legal proceeding during which evidence is presented, facts are determined by the jury, principles of law are applied, and a solution, or *verdict,* is reached

     e. Either the plaintiff or the defendant can appeal an unfavorable verdict to the appropriate appeals court, where the case is reviewed based on the trial record, the written summaries of the laws applied to the case, and the oral arguments of the attorneys

     f. *Execution of judgment* is made by the presiding judge when the appeals process is complete

3. Statute of limitations

     a. The *statute of limitations* specifies the time during which a plaintiff may file a lawsuit against a defendant to redress an injury or illegal act; after this time has elapsed, the lawsuit can never be filed again

     b. Most states allow 2 years as the filing period for a personal injury case

     c. The statute of limitations is strictly applied in traumatic injury cases because the patient would immediately know that injury has occurred

     d. The statute of limitations is applied less strictly in cases of illness or disease because of the time that can elapse before the patient becomes aware that malpractice has occurred

     e. In a case involving a minor, the statute of limitations begins when the minor reaches age 18, and the case must be filed before he reaches age 20

4. Expert witness

     a. An *expert witness* may be called by a lawyer to testify about matters that pertain to the witness's area of expertise (for example, to explain highly specialized technology to the judge and jury)

     b. To ensure objectivity, the expert witness should have no direct connection with the defendant or the plaintiff

     c. Testimony from an expert witness usually consists of opinions or responses to hypothetical questions

     d. Both the plaintiff and the defendant can retain expert witnesses

     e. When a nurse is the defendant, the ideal expert witness for the defense is another nurse with a similar level of education and experience

     f. A nurse who serves as an expert witness should be able to analyze the facts presented and draw inferences from those facts

## Points to Remember

All laws, regardless of origin, are subject to change and interpretation.

The legal system is based on four principles: a concern for justice and fairness, a need for laws to be pliable, application of similar standards of performance, and individual rights and responsibilities.

Every right granted to an individual has a corresponding responsibility, and failure to meet the responsibility can lead to a limitation of the right.

In a trial by jury, the jury is responsible for determining the facts of a case and making a decision based on those facts, and the judge is responsible for interpreting questions of law that apply to the case.

In a nonjury trial, the judge not only interprets questions of law but also determines the facts and makes a decision based on the facts.

A trial court, the first court to hear a case, is responsible for determining the facts of a case; an appeals court does not review the entire trial but accepts the determination of facts from the lower court and renders a decision based on the trial record.

The trial process follows a series of orderly steps to render a just decision.

The statute of limitations establishes a time limit for the filing of lawsuits and thus may prevent some cases from being tried if the time limit has expired.

Expert witnesses usually are asked to explain or offer opinions about highly technical skills or information.

## Glossary

**Appeal** — legal process by which a party dissatisfied with the decision of a lower court can seek a more favorable decision from a higher court

**Statute** — legislative act that declares, commands, or prohibits

# Nursing and the Law

**Learning Objectives**

After studying this section, the reader should be able to:

● Describe professional certification and its legal significance for nurses.

● List key elements commonly found in state nurse practice acts.

● Discuss the importance of scope of practice in nursing.

● Explain nursing liability, personal liability, employer liability, supervisor liability, dual employee liability, and charity immunity.

## VI. Nursing and the Law

A. **Introduction**
1. Nursing, like most health care professions, is highly regulated by the legal system to protect citizens from incompetent practitioners and other abuses within the health care system
2. Licensure is one method the state uses to establish a minimum level of competency for health care practitioners
3. The nurse practice act of each state outlines the requirements for licensing and the scope of practice for licensed nurses
4. State boards of nursing enforce nurse practice acts because state legislatures have neither the specialized knowledge nor the time required to perform this function (see Appendix D, United States Boards of Nursing, for more information); in Canada, the professional nurse association has the delegated authority to regulate nursing practice (see Appendix F, Canadian Nurses Association's Provincial and Territorial Members, for more information)
   a. A state board of nursing is created by definition in the state's nurse practice act
   b. The authority of each state board of nursing is granted by the state legislature
   c. Each nurse practice act establishes the number of board members, qualifications needed for membership, and length of time to be served
   d. The board has the authority to revoke or suspend professional licenses based on published guidelines and standards for professional behavior
5. Certification, another means of regulating health care professions, helps to maintain a high standard of care
   a. Certification is a professional credential that has no legal status unless defined in a nurse practice act
   b. Certification is granted to a nurse by a professional nursing organization, which issues a certificate recognizing that the nurse has met standards exceeding those required for the basic license
   c. Certification also can be granted for demonstrated excellence in direct patient care
   d. The requirements and methods for obtaining certification remain under the control of the organization granting the certification
   e. Certification for an expanded role in nursing can be legally sanctioned by the state board of nursing as recognition of competence in that role when the nurse practice act includes the role in its definition of scope of practice
   f. Expanded roles of a registered nurse that are legally recognized include nurse practitioner (NP), independent nurse practitioner (INP), family nurse practitioner (FNP), and pediatric nurse practitioner (PNP)
   g. Programs that prepare nurses for certification do not necessarily share the same standards for expected skills, and all states do not have the same requirements for certification, so transferring certifications from state to state can be difficult

6. The Joint Commission on Accreditation of Healthcare Organizations (JCAHO) is a means of regulating health care institutions
   a. The public wants health care institutions to have high professional standards
   b. The JCAHO establishes voluntary standards for the operation of health care institutions and the care of patients
   c. By meeting these standards, the hospital receives JCAHO accreditation (see Appendix G, Joint Commission on Accreditation of Healthcare Organizations Nursing Care Standards for more information)

## B. Nurse practice acts
1. General information
   a. A state nurse practice act is a legislative act that defines nursing practice and sets standards for the profession in that state
   b. These acts were originally designed to protect the public from incompetent or uneducated practitioners
   c. A nurse practice act includes general guidelines for acceptable actions of the professional nurse
   d. Although nurse practice acts vary in language and content from state to state (province to province in Canada), they share certain key elements
2. Common elements of nurse practice acts
   a. A definition of professional nursing (including nursing interventions and expanded professional functions)
   b. Requirements for licensure (including personal characteristics, educational requirements, passing score on the licensing examination, and citizenship) and possible exemptions from state licensure laws
   c. Requirements for relicensure, including those for voluntary or mandatory continuing education
   d. Definitions of reciprocity to recognize the equivalency of another state's license and board of nursing
   e. Means for disciplinary actions and requirements for due process of violations of the nurse practice act, including private reprimand or warning, public reprimand, probation, suspension of license, refusal to renew license, and license revocation
   f. Criteria for creating the state board of nursing and for designating members to serve on the board (usually from 5 to 10 members) so that all levels of nursing education and practice are represented
   g. Penalties for practicing without a license, including fines of $50 to $500 and imprisonment for up to 60 days
3. Scope of practice
   a. *Scope of practice,* as defined by each state's nurse practice act, outlines the activities a licensed nurse may legally perform when caring for patients in that state
   b. Nursing's scope of practice is flexible but has certain limits, depending primarily on the practice setting and the nurse's education and experience

      c.  An institution's manual of policies and procedures specifies the permissible scope of practice for nursing within a given setting in that institution; this scope of practice may be more narrow than — but cannot exceed — that described by the state nurse practice act

      d.  Each institution should periodically update the manual's definition of scope of practice to reflect changes in technology or nursing practice

      e.  A nurse who works outside the scope of nursing practice — as defined by the institution or the nurse practice act — is subject to legal action

  4.  Reporting violations of the nurse practice act

      a.  Most nurse practice acts legally require a nurse to report violations of the act

      b.  Common violations include drug abuse, intoxication at work, unprofessional conduct, actions that exceed the scope of practice, and criminal activities

      c.  The most appropriate way to report violations is through the institutional chain of command

      d.  Reports should be factual and well documented, including a complete description of the violation, a list of witnesses, specific dates and times of the incidents, and the names of patients involved

      e.  Supervisors and administrators of health care institutions are legally and ethically required to act on such reports

      f.  If the supervisors or administrators do not act on the report, the reporting nurse should take the issue to the state board of nursing

      g.  Anonymous reports are not accepted by state boards of nursing, but most state boards will protect the confidentiality of a nurse who signs a report

## C.  Nursing liability

  1.  General information

      a.  *Liability* refers to responsibility for one's actions

      b.  *Nursing liability* usually refers to a nurse's legal responsibility for harm caused to a patient by an inappropriate nursing action or by a failure to perform a required nursing action

      c.  A nurse cannot deny responsibility for a harmful act or inaction on the grounds that someone else was also responsible

      d.  For a nurse to be held legally liable, the nurse must have accepted the responsibility to provide competent nursing care according to the standards of care established for her profession, the patient must prove that the nurse failed to meet the required standards, a predictable potential for harm must be inherent in that failure, and actual harm must come to the patient as a direct result of the nurse's failure without any contributory act by the patient

  2.  Personal liability

      a.  *Personal liability* in nursing refers to a nurse's responsibility for nursing actions performed on the job

      b.  A nurse's personal liability increases proportionately to increases in education, experience, and skills

3. Employer liability
   a. *Employer liability* refers to an employer's responsibility for actions committed by its employees while on the job and emanates from the legal doctrine of *respondeat superior* ("let the master answer")
   b. As an employer, a hospital is responsible for hiring qualified, competent employees in sufficient numbers to meet staffing needs; ensuring a safe working environment, including safe, operable equipment; and providing adequate supervision of and direction for its employees
   c. Violation of one or more of these responsibilities can result in a lawsuit against the hospital
   d. To prove employer liability, an injured patient must show that the hospital had control over the nurse at the time of injury and that the injury occurred as a result of a negligent act within the course and scope of the nurse's job
   e. Employer liability never excuses a nurse from personal liability
4. Supervisor liability
   a. *Supervisor liability* refers to an employee's responsibility for the actions of subordinates
   b. A nurse supervisor is responsible for using sound judgment and making appropriate nursing decisions
   c. A nurse supervisor can be held legally liable for a subordinate's actions if they result from the supervisor's decisions and harm or injure a patient
   d. A nurse supervisor is not liable if the subordinate nurse's actions are proved to be beyond the limits of expected professional behavior
5. Dual employee liability
   a. *Dual employee liability* refers to the responsibility shared by two employees for the actions of one
   b. Two legal doctrines—*captain of the ship* and *borrowed servant*—usually apply to cases of dual employee liability (see Section VIII, Civil Liability, for more information on these doctrines)
   c. Dual employee liability can exist when a nurse employed by a hospital or other institution is directly supervised by a physician
   d. Such supervision must be immediate and must control the nurse's particular activities at the time of the injury or incident
   e. In cases of dual employee liability, a hospital is not liable for the negligent act of a nurse who followed the physician's orders
   f. The physician is liable for the actions of nurses under his direct supervision, even though he does not employ them
   g. The nurse still retains personal liability for all nursing actions
6. Charitable immunity
   a. *Charitable immunity* protects a nonprofit hospital from being held liable for harm done to patients
   b. Employees of charitable hospitals usually retain personal liability
   c. The current trend in legislatures and courts is to repeal blanket charitable immunity for institutions
   d. A nurse who works at a charitable institution should review state laws pertaining to charitable institutions and liability

## Points to Remember

A state board of nursing is granted authority by the state legislature to enforce the state's nurse practice act.

The scope of practice in nursing establishes the legal boundaries for professional practice as defined in the nurse practice act.

Nurses are legally required to report violations of the nurse practice act to an appropriate authority.

From a legal standpoint, the nurse fulfills three overlapping roles (provider of health care services, employee, and citizen), each of which carries with it legal rights and responsibilities.

Nursing liability in the legal system can involve personal liability, employer liability, supervisor liability, dual employee liability, and charitable immunity.

## Glossary

**Certification** — professional credential that acknowledges a higher level of skills in that profession; certification in nursing has no legal status unless defined in the nurse practice act of that state

**Due process** — specific procedures or steps one must follow to ensure a fair resolution of a conflict

**Liability** — legal responsibility for one's actions

**Nurse practice acts** — legislative acts that define nursing practice and set standards for the nursing profession in that state

**Scope of practice** — in nursing, activities that a licensed nurse may legally perform as defined in the nurse practice act

# Criminal Liability

**Learning Objectives**

After studying this section, the reader should be able to:

● Describe the elements necessary to convict a person of a crime.

● Discuss the significance of criminal law in society and health care.

● Distinguish between a felony and a misdemeanor.

● Identify the felonies and misdemeanors with which nurses are most likely to be involved in the work setting.

● Discuss ways in which criminal law violations apply to nursing.

## VII. Criminal Liability

### A. Introduction

1. *Criminal law* comprises all federal or state laws that affect the whole of society rather than the individual
   a. Because criminal laws affect all of society, the government is always the plaintiff in a criminal lawsuit
   b. Congress has the right (through the power granted to it by the people) to declare which acts are crimes when those acts involve the federal government
   c. Each state identifies crimes within its own jurisdiction based on public policy and the people's will
2. A *crime* is a criminal act (in violation of criminal law) made with criminal intent; a person cannot be convicted of a crime unless both elements exist
   a. A *criminal act (actus reas)* is either an act that the law forbids or omission of an act that the law requires
   b. *Criminal intent (mens reas)* refers to the state of mind of one who commits a criminal act despite knowing that it is against the law
   c. Crimes are classified as felonies or misdemeanors, depending on their severity
3. A jury may find that a defendant did not have criminal intent if:
   a. The act was involuntary or accidental
   b. The defendant (such as a mentally impaired person) could not understand that the act was criminal
   c. The act was necessary (such as an act of self-defense)
4. After a verdict has been rendered in a trial, both sides have a right to appeal the verdict to the intermediate and ultimate courts of appeal in the appropriate legal system
5. A person who has been tried on a criminal charge cannot be tried again for the same criminal charge
6. Punishment for a crime has two goals: to protect society from the offender and to deter others from committing the same crime
7. Forms of punishment for conviction of a crime include:
   a. Monetary fine
   b. Loss of privileges, such as loss of a nursing license
   c. Parole
   d. Imprisonment
   e. Execution
8. A crime can result in a civil lawsuit as well as a criminal case
9. A professional who commits a crime for which he is not prosecuted still can lose his job, have his license revoked, and suffer damage to his reputation
10. Nurses are subject to criminal liability
    a. Violation of any law governing the practice of any licensed profession may be a crime under the profession's practice act

b. The two most common nurse-related violations of criminal law involve the state nurse practice act (punishable by suspension or probation) and safe nursing practices, such as medication errors or termination of life-support without an order (punishable by fine or imprisonment and loss of license)

## B. Felonies
1. General information
   a. A *felony* usually refers to any serious criminal offense; the U.S. legal system lacks a more specific definition
   b. Felonies are declared by statute or by common law; all other crimes are classified as misdemeanors
   c. Punishment for conviction of a felony can be a fine of $1,000 or more, imprisonment for 1 year or more, or death
2. Nursing-related felonies
   a. *Murder* is the unlawful killing of another person with malice aforethought (nurses at a Veterans Administration hospital in Michigan were convicted of murder after they injected pancuronium bromide [Pavulon] into patients' intravenous infusions, and a California nurse was convicted of murdering 12 elderly patients with massive doses of lidocaine [Xylocaine])
   b. *Manslaughter* is the killing of another person without malice aforethought and may or may not be a felony, depending on the circumstances (a New Jersey nurse was convicted of manslaughter after a patient died from an incompatible blood transfusion; the nurse disposed of the remaining blood and altered the patient's medical records, supporting the inference of criminal intent)
   c. *Assault* is a threat to inflict physical injury on another person through force or violence, and *battery* is an assault in which any force, however slight, is applied to another (for instance, a nurse could be convicted of assault for unnecessarily threatening to use leather restraints on a patient and could be convicted of battery for using the restraints; assault and battery may be considered misdemeanors rather than felonies if the force or violence used is slight)
   d. *Kidnapping* is the holding, seizing, or carrying off of another person against his will by force or fraud (such as committing a patient to a mental institution against his will without a medically justifiable cause)
   e. A *controlled substance violation* usually is considered a felony only when it involves an intent to sell illegal drugs or when another felony is committed (such as stealing a narcotic from a supply cabinet and selling the drug)
3. Application to nursing
   a. Like any other citizen, a nurse who violates criminal law can be tried for a felony

      b. A felony conviction in most states will lead to revocation or suspension of the nurse's license

      c. A harmful act committed by a nurse in the health care setting would not be considered a felony unless it was extremely harmful, showed evidence of intent to commit a crime, or displayed gross negligence that resulted in significant physical injury (for example, intentionally shutting off a ventilator without permission)

## C. Misdemeanors

1. General information

      a. A *misdemeanor* usually refers to any crime not classified as a felony by statute or common law

      b. Punishment for conviction of a misdemeanor can be a fine of less than $1,000, imprisonment in a local jail for less than 1 year, or both

      c. A crime that usually is classified as a misdemeanor may be considered a felony if the evidence shows sufficient criminal intent and significant harm to an individual or society

2. Nursing-related misdemeanors

      a. *Criminally negligent involuntary manslaughter* is the unintentional killing of another person through a failure to act when one has a duty to act to prevent death (for example, if a nurse fails to provide care for an obviously sick child who subsequently dies)

      b. *Unlawful act involuntary manslaughter* is the unintentional killing of another person through commission of an unlawful act (for example, if a nurse attempts to carry out a surgical procedure that causes a patient's death)

      c. *Failure to report certain injuries or illnesses* (such as a gunshot wound, rape, a sexually transmitted disease, and child abuse) can result in a misdemeanor charge against a health professional

      d. *Failure to provide emergency services* can constitute a misdemeanor if the hospital's failure is willful and causes injury to a patient

      e. *Fraudulent business activities* (such as forgery, embezzlement, and receiving stolen property) are misdemeanors that sometimes involve hospitals, physicians, nurses (especially those with independent practices), and other health care personnel

      f. *Violations of professional practice acts or health and safety codes* constitute misdemeanors when they injure or harm a person or his property (such as a nurse who prescribes medicine or knowingly uses defective equipment)

3. Application to nursing

      a. Most crimes committed by nurses in the health care setting are misdemeanors

b. The most common offense is a violation of the nurse practice act (such as practicing without a current license, engaging in activities outside the scope of nursing practice, or aiding others in the illegal practice of medicine)

c. The second most common offense is a violation of the narcotic laws (such as using, selling, or illegally distributing controlled substances or stealing drugs from a hospital)

d. Assault and battery charges can be filed against a nurse if the nurse treats a patient who refuses health care, especially when such treatments are considered routine (such as blood transfusions, tube feedings, fluid administration, and certain life-support treatments)

e. To guard against false accusations of criminal liability in the health care setting, a nurse should know and obey all federal and state laws that pertain to nursing, abide by the nurse practice act, and keep thorough and accurate patient records

## Points to Remember

To be convicted of a crime, one must commit a criminal act with criminal intent.

Crimes are classified as felonies or misdemeanors.

Most crimes committed by nurses on the job are considered misdemeanors.

Violations of the nurse practice act and narcotic laws are the two most common criminal charges brought against nurses in the work setting.

## Glossary

**Malice aforethought** — intent to commit an unlawful act

**Verdict** — formal decision rendered by a jury in a trial

# Civil Liability

**Learning Objectives**

After studying this section, the reader should be able to:

● Discuss the significance of civil law in society and health care.

● Define tort.

● Define and explain unintentional, intentional, and quasi-intentional torts.

● Identify the major acts in each tort category that constitute civil law violations.

## VIII. Civil Liability

### A. Introduction

1. *Civil law* comprises all laws that affect the individual rather than the whole of society
2. Civil law is administered by individuals rather than by the government
   a. In a civil lawsuit, the person who files the claim is the *plaintiff* or *petitioner,* and the person against whom the claim is made is the *defendant* or *respondent*
   b. Civil law violations are punishable by damages, usually in the form of monetary compensation to the plaintiff from the defendant (see "Malpractice," page 69, for more detailed information)
   c. The jury or judge determines the amount of compensation
   d. Civil courts do not impose fines or prison sentences but may rule that a person who violates a civil law must perform a specific action, such as service to the community
3. The four types of civil law are contract law, labor law, patent law, and tort law
4. Lawsuits that involve nursing and health care commonly fall under tort law
5. A *tort* is a wrongful act committed against a person or his property independent of a contract
   a. A person who commits a tort is liable for damages to those wrongfully injured
   b. A tort may constitute a direct invasion of a person's legal right, a violation of a public or private duty that damages a person, or a combination of these
   c. Torts are of three types: unintentional, intentional, and quasi-intentional (see *Selected Tort Claims,* page 68)

### B. Unintentional torts

1. General information
   a. An *unintentional tort* is a wrongful, albeit unintended, act against another person or his property
   b. Unintentional torts are commonly regarded as acts of negligence
2. Negligence
   a. *Negligence* is the omission of an act that a reasonable and prudent person would perform in a similar situation guided by considerations that ordinarily regulate human affairs
   b. Negligence is based on four doctrines of liability: master-servant, the twin doctrines of borrowed servant and captain of the ship, ostensible agency, and res ipsa loquitur
   c. According to the *master-servant doctrine* (also called *respondeat superior,* "let the master answer"), an employer is also liable, along with an employee, for the employee's negligence on the job

## SELECTED TORT CLAIMS

Like all health care professionals, nurses are vulnerable to lawsuits. A patient who feels that nursing care is inappropriate might file a lawsuit claiming one of the six torts selected below. This chart shows intentional, quasi-intentional, and unintentional torts and some examples of improper nursing actions that could lead a patient to use each claim in a lawsuit.

| TORT CLAIMS | IMPROPER NURSING ACTION |
|---|---|
| **UNINTENTIONAL TORT** | |
| Malpractice | • Leaving foreign objects inside a patient following surgery<br>• Failing to observe a patient as the doctor ordered<br>• Failing to ensure a patient's informed consent<br>• Failing to report a change in a patient's vital signs or status<br>• Failing to report a fellow staff member's negligence<br>• Failing to provide for a patient's safety<br>• Failing to provide the patient with sufficient and appropriate teaching before discharge |
| **INTENTIONAL TORTS** | |
| Assault | • Threatening a patient |
| Battery | • Forcing a patient to ambulate against his wishes<br>• Forcing a patient to submit to injections<br>• Striking a patient |
| False imprisonment | • Confining a patient in a psychiatric unit without a doctor's order<br>• Refusing to let a patient return home |
| **QUASI-INTENTIONAL TORTS** | |
| Invasion of privacy | • Releasing private information about a patient to a third party<br>• Allowing an unauthorized person to read a patient's medical records<br>• Allowing an unauthorized person to observe a procedure<br>• Taking pictures of a patient who has not given consent |
| Slander | • Making false statements about a patient to news reporters |
| Libel | • Writing in the chart that a patient is a homosexual |

d. According to the *borrowed servant* and *captain of the ship* doctrines, a nurse employed by a hospital is a temporary servant or agent of the physician, an independent contractor who directly supervises the nurse; thus, the physician and the nurse are liable for the nurse's negligence, but the hospital is not

      e.  According to the *ostensible agency doctrine,* a hospital or other health care agency may be held liable for the negligence of a nonemployee (such as an independent agent or contractor) if either the person or the agency has represented or implied to the public that the person was an employee and the patient relied on that fact when seeking care at the agency

      f.  According to the doctrine of *res ipsa loquitur* ("let the thing speak for itself"), a negligent act can be proved by circumstantial evidence, without all the required elements of liability, if the nature of the incident and the circumstances surrounding it show that the injury would not have occurred without the negligence; this doctrine sometimes applies when a patient was in surgery or otherwise unconscious during care

  3.  Malpractice

      a.  *Malpractice,* a form of negligence, is the failure of a professional to act as a reasonable and prudent professional with the same education and experience would have acted in a similar situation

      b.  One must be a professional (a member of a profession whose practice is regulated by the government through an administrative agency) to be sued for malpractice; otherwise, such misconduct is classified as negligence

      c.  Malpractice implies that a professional is held to a higher standard than a nonprofessional would be

      d.  Malpractice can involve professional misconduct, unreasonable lack of skill or fidelity in professional duties, evil practice, or illegal or immoral conduct

      e.  To prove liability on the part of a health professional, a patient must prove that a duty was owed to the patient, that the professional violated the duty, that the professional could have foreseen the harm that might result, that the patient was injured or harmed, and that the professional's negligence caused the harm

      f.  A health professional found guilty of malpractice may have to provide monetary compensation to the patient for *general damages* that are a direct outcome of the injury (such as pain, suffering, disability, and disfigurement), *special damages* that result from the injury (such as medical bills and lost wages), *optional damages* that are an outgrowth of the initial injury (such as emotional diseases, mental suffering, and counseling expenses), and *punitive* or *exemplary damages* if the patient proves that the professional acted with conscious disregard for the patient's safety in a malicious, willful, or wanton manner

## C.  Intentional torts

  1.  General information

      a.  An *intentional tort* is a willful act that violates another person's rights or property

b. To be considered intentional, a tort must include three elements: the defendant's act must be intended to interfere with the plaintiff or his property, the defendant must intend to bring about the consequences of the act, and the act must be a substantial factor in causing the consequences

c. To prove the defendant's liability in an intentional tort case, the plaintiff does not have to prove that damages or injury occurred; proof of the defendant's intentional interference with the plaintiff's person or property is sufficient

d. A patient does not have to provide expert witnesses to prove an intentional tort claim against a health care provider

e. Punitive damages are more likely to be assessed against a defendant in an intentional tort case than in a case of negligence

f. An intentional tort may fall under the jurisdiction of a criminal court if the act is extreme and demonstrates gross violations of standards of care and practice

2. Assault
   a. *Assault* is an act that causes another person to fear that he will be touched in an offensive, insulting, or physically injurious manner without consent or authority, such as raising a fist in a threatening way
   b. A verbal threat to touch someone in this manner also is an assault, even though physical contact does not follow, such as threatening to inject a disruptive patient with a sedative

3. Battery
   a. *Battery* is harmful or unwarranted contact with a person without his consent
   b. Health care personnel who perform surgery on a patient without his consent can be charged with battery

4. False imprisonment
   a. *False imprisonment* is the illegal detention of a person without his consent
   b. Using physical restraints, threats, or medications to treat a patient without his consent can constitute false imprisonment

5. Intentional infliction of emotional distress
   a. *Intentional infliction of emotional distress* is the use of extreme conduct to cause severe emotional distress to another
   b. A person who is charged with assault, battery, or false imprisonment can also be charged with infliction of emotional distress

## D. Quasi-intentional torts
1. General information
   a. A *quasi-intentional tort* is a voluntary act that directly causes injury or distress without intent to injure or distress
   b. A quasi-intentional tort violates a person's reputation, personal privacy, civil rights, or freedom from malicious or unfounded prosecution

2. Defamation of character
   a. *Defamation of character* is an invasion of a person's reputation and good name and comprises the twin torts of slander and libel
   b. *Slander* is a false oral statement that unjustly damages a person's reputation (a nurse who fabricates medical information about a patient when conversing with a coworker could be held liable for slander)
   c. *Libel* is a false written or representational statement (words, cartoons, or effigies) that unjustly damages a person's reputation (a nurse who includes unfounded or irrelevant personal information about a patient in his chart can be charged with libel)
   d. Defamation injures a person's reputation by diminishing the esteem, respect, goodwill, or confidence that others have for him and can be especially damaging when false statements are made about a criminal or immoral act or a contagious or dreaded disease
   e. To win a defamation of character lawsuit against a nurse, the patient must prove that the nurse acted in malice, abused the principle of privileged communication (in which certain types of communication between professionals or organizations are confidential and cannot be made public), and wrote or spoke an untruth
3. Invasion of privacy
   a. *Invasion of privacy* is a violation of a person's right to protection against unreasonable and unwarranted interference with his personal life
   b. To prove invasion of privacy, a patient must show that a health care worker intruded into the patient's seclusion, that a reasonable and prudent patient would object to the intrusion, that the health care worker pried into the patient's private information, and that the private information was publicly disclosed
   c. Examples of invading a patient's privacy include using the patient's name or picture for the sole advantage of the health care practitioner, intruding into the patient's private affairs without permission, or publishing information that misrepresents the patient or his condition
4. Breach of confidentiality
   a. *Breach of confidentiality* is a type of invasion of privacy in which a person's trust and confidence are violated by public revelation of confidential or privileged communications without the person's consent
   b. Breach of confidentiality usually involves a physician's revelation of communications with a patient but can also extend to nurses who share privileged communication or information
5. Malicious prosecution
   a. *Malicious prosecution* refers to a situation in which a person is forced to be a defendant in a legal action when no foundation for the action exists
   b. A person can prove malicious prosecution only if he was found innocent in the original trial, the court action against him was initiated without sufficient and probable cause, the court action was conducted with malice, and he was forced to pay damages to the plaintiff or suffered harm to his reputation as a result of the case

    c. Malicious prosecution cases are difficult to win, especially in proving that the original court action was conducted with malice

6. Civil rights violations

    a. A *civil rights violation* is a wrongful act against another person that violates a civil rights statute

    b. The most common civil rights violations in the health care setting involve an administration's decisions about hiring or terminating employees; disputes over due process, such as committing a patient to a mental health facility without following the proper procedure; and an institution's provision of care based on sex, race, or creed

    c. Civil rights cases sometimes fall under the jurisdiction of the criminal courts

    d. A civil rights violation is the least frequent type of tort brought against health care providers

## Points to Remember

Most legal actions brought against nurses are civil lawsuits that fall under tort law.

Intentional and quasi-intentional torts can be tried in the criminal justice system if they are extreme and gross violations of care and practice.

## Glossary

**Intentional tort**—willful act that violates another person's rights or property

**Malpractice**—failure of a professional to act as a reasonable and prudent professional with the same education and experience would have acted in a similar situation

**Quasi-intentional tort**—voluntary act that directly causes injury or distress without intent to injure or distress

**Tort**—wrongful act committed against a person or his property independent of a contract

**Unintentional tort**—wrongful, albeit unintended, act against another person or his property

# Professional Licensure in Nursing

**Learning Objectives**

After studying this section, the reader should be able to:

- Define licensure and discuss its primary purposes.

- Distinguish mandatory licensure from permissive licensure.

- List the customary exemptions to mandatory licensure.

- Define institutional licensure and explain why professionals usually oppose it.

## IX. Professional Licensure in Nursing

### A. Introduction

1. Many health care practitioners — including professional nurses, technical nurses, respiratory therapists, and physical therapists — are required to obtain a license to practice their skills

2. *Licensure* refers to the legal process by which a designated authority grants permission to a qualified individual to perform designated skills and services in a given jurisdiction

   a. Licensure is a function of the state (in Canada, the province), arising from the state's obligation to protect its citizens from incompetent or unsafe health care practitioners

   b. The state (or province) in which a nurse lives is the authority that grants the nurse permission to practice

### B. Types of nursing licensure

1. Professional licensure

   a. *Professional licensure* is a legal method to control the quality of a profession by establishing a minimum level of competency for a professional to be licensed

   b. The state board of nursing grants professional licensure to nurses

   c. Professional licensing laws are contained within the nurse practice act of each state (see *U.S. and Canadian Licensing Laws*)

## U.S. AND CANADIAN LICENSING LAWS

| U.S. LICENSING LAWS | CANADIAN LICENSING LAWS |
|---|---|
| Licensing laws are contained within each state's nurse practice act. They establish qualifications for obtaining and maintaining a nursing license and broadly define the legally permissible scope of nursing practice. Although licensing laws may vary from state to state, they usually specify the following: | Each province has its own nurse practice act, so laws may vary from province to province. Licensing laws in all provinces, except Prince Edward Island and Ontario, require nurses to join provincial nursing associations in order to obtain their licenses. In all provinces, Canadian nursing laws establish the following: |
| • qualifications required to obtain a license<br>• application procedures for new licenses and reciprocal licensing arrangements<br>• application fees<br>• authorization to grant the use of the title of registered nurse<br>• grounds for license denial, revocation, or suspension<br>• license renewal procedures | • qualifications for membership in the provincial nursing association<br>• examination requirements<br>• application fees<br>• conditions for reciprocal licensure<br>• penalties for practicing without a license<br>• grounds for denial, suspension, or revocation of a nurse's license |

    d. To obtain a professional nursing license, a nurse must meet certain requirements, including completion of a state board-approved nursing school program, payment of a fee designated by the state, and satisfactory completion of the National Council Licensure Examination for Registered Nurses (NCLEX-RN)

    e. Some nonprofessionals view professional licensure as a means to obtain economic and vocational security

2. Institutional licensure

    a. *Institutional licensure* refers to the process by which a state government regulates institutions that provide health care services

    b. Institutional licensure grants the institution the authority to regulate certain aspects of care, including the practice of staff members, administration and staffing requirements, equipment specifications, and safety regulations

    c. Professional organizations usually oppose institutional licensure because it gives the institution, rather than the profession, the right to regulate the professional's practice

3. Mandatory licensure

    a. *Mandatory licensure* refers to the legal requirement of a person earning compensation as a member of a licensed profession to obtain a license to use the title of a profession and to practice the skills or services of the profession

    b. All states have some form of mandatory licensure

    c. Exemptions to mandatory nursing licensure permit an unlicensed person to perform nursing actions in certain circumstances

    d. Those exempted from mandatory nursing licensure include any unlicensed person during an emergency, a student nurse during her course of study, a federal government employee who is licensed in another jurisdiction, a graduate nurse during the time between taking the NCLEX-RN and obtaining results of the exam, and a licensed nurse helping to transport a patient through a state outside the jurisdiction of the nurse's license

4. Permissive licensure

    a. *Permissive licensure* regulates use of professional titles rather than professional actions

    b. Only persons who pass the NCLEX-RN can use the title of registered nurse (RN)

    c. Under permissive licensure, a person without the title of RN can perform many nursing actions of an RN when supervised in an appropriate setting

    d. Permissive licensure has the potential for abuse because a person without the appropriate educational background can continue to perform nursing actions as long as the person does not claim the title of RN

    e. Only Texas and the District of Columbia have permissive licensure

## Points to Remember

Professional licensure is a function of the state, arising from the state's obligation to protect its citizens from incompetent or unsafe health care practitioners.

Licensure establishes a minimum level of competency.

Institutional licensure allows institutions to regulate the standards of a profession and is usually opposed by all professional organizations.

All states have some form of mandatory licensure.

Permissive licensure has the potential for abuse because it allows professional activities to be performed by individuals who may not have the appropriate education to do so.

## Glossary

**Institutional licensure** — process by which a state government regulates institutions that provide health care services

**Licensure** — legal process by which a designated authority grants permission to a qualified individual to perform designated skills and services in a given jurisdiction

**Mandatory licensure** — legal requirement of a person who is earning compensation as a member of a licensed profession to obtain a license to use the title of the profession and to practice the skills and services of the profession

**Mandatory nursing licensure exemptions** — statements in the nurse practice act that permit unlicensed individuals, such as student nurses, to perform nursing actions in certain situations

**Permissive licensure** — form of licensure that regulates the use of professional titles rather than professional actions

**Professional licensure** — legal method to control the quality of a profession by establishing a minimum level of competency for a professional to be licensed

# Legally Sensitive Practice Settings

**Learning Objectives**

After studying this section, the reader should be able to:

● Identify nursing practice settings that have a high potential for legal actions against nurses.

● List the most common types of negligence and other tort claims made against nurses in each setting.

● Identify key legal doctrines that apply to the various practice settings.

● Discuss the implications for nurses who work in each setting if they are to avoid legal action.

## X. Legally Sensitive Practice Settings

### A. Introduction

1. With increasing frequency, nurses are being named as defendants or co-defendants in malpractice lawsuits
2. In an era of cost containment, hospitals and other health care agencies are less willing to assume sole responsibility for the negligence of their employees
3. Although many nursing errors can be made in virtually any practice setting, nurses who work in certain practice settings are more vulnerable to malpractice charges because their errors can prove more costly for patients

### B. Critical care unit

1. General information
   a. Nearly 5,000 hospitals in the United States have some type of critical care unit
   b. Critical care units can include those for coronary care, general medicine, surgery, neonatology, neurology, neurosurgery, pediatrics, cardiac surgery, burns, respiratory disorders, or a combination of any of the above
   c. Smaller hospitals tend to have combined critical care units, whereas larger hospitals usually have separate specialty units
   d. Compared to other hospital units, critical care units have a larger nursing staff and a higher nurse-patient ratio (usually one nurse for every two or three patients)
   e. Compared to nurses in other units, critical care nurses spend proportionately more of their time in direct contact with their patients, thus increasing the opportunity for error and the number of potential lawsuits
   f. Critical care units have the latest advances in technology and tend to use complex, sophisticated equipment in the everyday care of patients, thus increasing the complexity of care and nursing responsibilities
   g. Nurses are responsible for learning to operate this equipment and to recognize equipment malfunction
   h. Incorrect operation or malfunction of life-sustaining equipment can result in death or significant harm to patients
   i. All critical care units, no matter what the specialty, combine intensive nursing care with high technology and constant monitoring of patients
   j. Critical care nurses provide continuous and intensive care for patients who have acute, life-threatening diseases or injuries
   k. Critical care nurses assume the primary responsibility for implementing and supporting the intensive treatment of life-threatening ailments

l. Critical care nurses must have a thorough knowledge of medical and surgical practices, medication actions and effects, and normal and abnormal laboratory results and must be able to perform thorough physical assessments and interpret the results

m. Critical care nurses must be proficient in various technical skills because they are required to take quick action in a life-threatening emergency

n. Critical care nurses are especially vulnerable to charges of negligence or battery because of the many invasive and potentially harmful procedures performed in their setting

o. A written policy that stipulates the guidelines to follow when performing procedures in the critical care unit provides effective legal protection for the nurse

2. Sources of legal action

a. A nurse who undertakes responsibilities without specific regulatory authorization is violating the scope of nursing practice

b. A scope of practice violation usually is a criminal matter (violation of the state nurse practice act) but also can fall under the jurisdiction of civil law

c. Critical care nurses are sometimes accused of practicing medicine without a license when they perform expanded role duties and procedures

d. Scope of practice violations can be avoided if a physician properly delegates to a qualified nurse the authority to implement a particular treatment

e. Failure to meet published standards of care is a potential foundation for a lawsuit; standards for critical care nurses are established by the American Association of Critical Care Nurses

f. The courts may expect a higher standard of practice from a nurse who practices in a specialty area and are more likely to impose a higher standard of care on a nurse with certification in a specialty area

g. The practice of *floating* nurses from other units to fill in for shortages in critical care units may increase the potential for lawsuits against nurses and hospitals

h. Critical care nurses are more vulnerable to charges of *abandonment* because of their obligation to observe patients closely for any subtle changes in condition

i. Medication errors in the critical care setting can be devastating—even lethal—to a patient; to claim that "the physician ordered it" is an unacceptable defense for a nurse

j. Failure to follow an established unit policy or protocol is a breach of the standards of care established by a hospital and, as such, is difficult to defend in court

k. Failure to obtain informed consent is more likely to occur in a critical care setting because of the inherent pressure and urgency for immediate treatment

      l. Wrongful treatment involving invasion of privacy, intentional infliction of emotional distress, battery, or a civil rights violation has a higher probability of occurring in a critical care unit, especially if the case involves a patient who was placed on or removed from a life-support system

      m. Battery could be upheld for wrongful treatment if a competent patient refuses treatment and the treatment is continued anyway

      n. Critical care nurses who deny a competent patient the right to refuse treatment — even if lack of treatment results in the patient's death — expose themselves to charges of various intentional torts and perhaps criminal actions

  3. Implications for nurses

      a. The increasing responsibilities of critical care nurses may result in more lawsuits being brought against them

      b. To maintain an autonomous professional standard of care, critical care nurses must insist that expert witnesses called to judge their practice have similar knowledge and skills and are familiar with practice in similar circumstances

      c. All professionals, including nurses, have a legal obligation to know the limits of their knowledge and skills; thus, an inexperienced nurse who is asked to work in a critical care unit should decline the assignment

      d. Any institution with a critical care unit has an obligation to provide adequate preparation and training for employees who are asked to work in the unit

      e. Nurses have an obligation to know the critical care unit's policies and procedures because failure to follow these can lead to an indefensible lawsuit

      f. Critical care nurses need to understand the philosophical issues involved in do-not-resuscitate (DNR) orders and should work to institute clear and realistic policies they can follow

      g. Becoming certified as a critical care nurse (CCRN) is one step a nurse can take to ensure adequate knowledge in this area

## C. Emergency department

  1. General information

      a. Patients' use of emergency departments is increasing dramatically throughout the United States

      b. Patients seek treatment at emergency departments not only for emergencies (such as myocardial infarction and acute trauma) but also for routine health problems (such as colds, flu, and minor injuries)

      c. Emergency departments sometimes serve as a physician's office for people who do not have or cannot afford a primary physician

    d. The emergency department nurse has become a specialty practitioner and can obtain certification in emergency nursing by successfully completing the certification examination offered by the Emergency Nurses Association (ENA)

    e. Emergency departments in some large hospitals have developed subspecialty emergency units to treat specific conditions, such as cardiac arrest, gunshot and knife wounds, and drug overdoses

    f. Liability for emergency department nurses may involve negligence, intentional torts, or civil rights violations

    g. Many of the day-to-day practices of emergency department nurses fall into a legal gray area because the law's definition of a *true emergency* is open to interpretations; for instance, health care workers who treat a patient for what they regard as a true emergency may be liable for battery or failure to obtain informed consent if the court ultimately concludes that the situation was not a true emergency

    h. According to common law, a health care provider has no duty to render assistance to a person who needs medical care, even in an emergency, unless the provider has already agreed to render such care or the person's condition resulted from the provider's actions

    i. *Good Samaritan laws* provide immunity from civil liability for any act or omission of an act by a person who provides emergency care in good faith and without compensation at the scene of an emergency

    j. Unless otherwise specified in a statute, Good Samaritan laws do not apply to nurses working in hospital emergency departments, on rescue teams, or in mobile emergency care units because these nurses usually are paid for their services, are not at the scene of the emergency, or both

    k. A hospital that advertises emergency care facilities or receives federal funds for maintaining such facilities is obligated to provide emergency care for anyone who enters the facilities

    l. According to the standards of care established by the Emergency Nurses Association, an emergency department nurse is required to assess a patient's condition, institute appropriate care to stabilize the patient, and prevent complications

2. Sources of legal action

    a. Failure to assess and report a patient's condition is one of the most common charges filed against emergency department nurses and sometimes involves a failure to recognize an obstetrical, pediatric, or psychiatric emergency

    b. The use of high-tech equipment in acute and typically hectic situations increases the potential for lawsuits against emergency department nurses

    c. Inadequate triage (a nurse's failure to recognize potential dangers to a patient and to respond appropriately) can be considered negligence

    d. A nurse who discounts complaints of pain from a patient who is mentally impaired by alcohol, medication, or injury—particularly if the complaints are not directly related to evident injuries—is vulnerable to legal action

    e. Because many patients go home after spending only a short time in the emergency department, emergency nurses are at an increased risk for failure to instruct a patient adequately before discharge

    f. Because of the serious, sometimes invasive treatments required in emergency departments, nurses in this setting are subject to increased liability for failure to obtain informed consent, battery, false imprisonment, and invasions of privacy

    g. Under some state statutes, emergency department nurses can be held liable for failure to report certain crimes or suspected crimes, including child abuse, knife or gun wounds, battery, and rape

    h. Emergency department nurses also may become involved in liability cases if they are asked or ordered by police to obtain evidence to be used in prosecuting a patient or another person

    i. An emergency department nurse's liability for performing certain actions (such as drawing blood to determine alcohol and drug levels, performing catheterization for similar tests, and taking pictures to confirm suspected child abuse) depends on the laws of the state in which the nurse practices; for example, taking blood samples by invasive measures against a patient's wishes usually constitutes battery

3. Implications for nurses

    a. Nurses who practice in emergency departments must have wide-ranging skills, from acute emergency care to ambulatory and routine care

    b. Emergency department nurses should be aware of the traditional principles of professional negligence

    c. Detailed documentation is required in all emergencies, including the triage note stating when the patient arrived, his condition on arrival, an initial assessment of vital signs, the chief complaint, and a brief review of systems

    d. The emergency nurse should be familiar with the state nurse practice act and any administrative regulations that govern emergency nursing practice

    e. A nurse's independent duty to a patient arises from the privilege of licensure—not from the hospital's requirement to treat the patient or the physician's relationship to the patient; thus, a nurse is required to care for a patient regardless of the patient's relationship with the hospital

    f. Emergency department nurses are obligated to listen to and assess the validity of all patient complaints, regardless of the patient's mental status

    g. Written instructions to patients are more thorough and easier to document—and thus give the nurse greater legal protection—than oral instructions

    h. Emergency department nurses should be involved in the development of policies and procedures regarding the handling and obtaining of evidence, mandatory reporting, and written instructions

    i. Nurses must be thoroughly familiar with departmental policies to aid them in exercising sound judgment during emergencies

    j. Instructions to discharged patients should include a list of the potential dangers of not following the instructions or not seeking additional medical attention

    k. Becoming certified as an emergency nurse (CEN) is one step a nurse can take to ensure adequate knowledge in this area

## D. Psychiatric unit

  1. General information

    a. Before the 1960s, little legal protection was given to the psychiatric patient, and little legal liability was demanded from the psychiatric nurse

    b. Current legal thinking affords the psychiatric patient the same rights given to patients in other care settings

    c. Most court cases involving psychiatric nurses revolve around a violation of one or more of these patients' rights

    d. Negligence cases involving medication or other treatment errors occur in the psychiatric setting, but with much less frequency

    e. The practice setting for psychiatric and mental health nursing is varied, embracing hospitals, outpatient clinics, and private offices

    f. Psychiatric nurses can assume various roles, from a unit nurse in a large hospital to an independent psychiatric practitioner in a nurse-run clinic

    g. Many state codes have been developed to address admission and discharge procedures from psychiatric institutions

    h. *Voluntary admission* is one in which a patient admits himself for a specific time for a specific type of treatment

    i. Voluntary admission is desirable because it allows a patient to make decisions about treatment and to seek discharge when he feels ready to go home

    j. *Involuntary admission* is one initiated by someone other than the patient and results in many restrictions on the patient's individual rights

    k. Most states have specific due process procedures governing involuntary admissions to psychiatric institutions

    l. The underlying assumption of these procedures is that a mentally ill patient either can be reasonably expected to inflict serious harm to himself or others in the near future or cannot provide for his basic needs in a way that will prevent serious harm

    m. Emergency involuntary admission, typically initiated by a law officer or family member, occurs when a patient is in immediate need of hospitalization

    n. An emergency patient must have a psychiatric examination within 72 hours of admission, with a statement by a certified examiner that the patient requires hospitalization

    o. A court order must be obtained for involuntary admissions to psychiatric hospitals in nonemergencies

    p. The mandate of the *least restrictive alternative treatment* states that a patient should be treated in a setting that results in the least restrictions on his liberty and freedom

    q. A mentally ill patient is presumed by the courts to be mentally competent and therefore able to give consent for treatment while hospitalized

2. Sources of legal action

    a. Violation of a patient's right to treatment after involuntary admission to a psychiatric institution violates the Eighth Amendment right to protection against cruel and unusual punishment

    b. Failure to obtain informed consent can occur in the psychiatric setting, often unintentionally, especially if the patient's condition interferes with his awareness or understanding of the proposed treatment or procedure

    c. Violation of a patient's right to refuse treatment usually stems from a mistaken belief that all mentally ill patients are incompetent; the right to refuse treatment is not absolute, however, and can be abrogated if medications or treatments are required to prevent serious harm to the patient or others

    d. Violation of a patient's right to privacy and confidentiality — such as revealing personal information about a patient to someone not directly involved in his care — is a common complaint in lawsuits against psychiatric health care workers, probably because of the stigma still associated with seeking care for mental illness

    e. Failure to protect a patient from inflicting foreseeable harm to himself or others not only violates his right to a safe environment but also may violate the nurse's duty to assess and report his condition if the nurse fails to report information given by the patient, even in confidence, that could have prevented the harm

3. Implications for nurses

    a. Psychiatric nurses are held to the same standards of reasonable and prudent behavior expected of other professionals with the same education in similar circumstances and must provide care that meets the professional standards established by the American Nurse's Association (ANA)

    b. Psychiatric nurses must know and abide by statutory provisions concerning patient admissions into psychiatric care

    c. Obtaining informed consent is the physician's responsibility, but the nurse should supply the patient with relevant information about consent and document whether or not the consent was valid

d. A nurse who must violate a patient's rights, for whatever reason, should carefully document all signs and symptoms, treatments, and treatment effects as a precaution against litigation

e. A nurse can legally use restraints or seclusion, if clinically necessary, to protect a patient's right to a safe environment

f. Because of the obligation to prevent a patient from inflicting harm to himself, even against his wishes, psychiatric nurses must be particularly cautious when caring for suicidal patients

## E. Obstetrical unit

1. General information

   a. Obstetrical nurses provide wide-ranging services and care for maternal patients in and out of the hospital

   b. Monetary damages for wrongful incidents in the obstetrical unit tend to be large because of the permanent or long-term injuries that occur to newborns

   c. Cases involving obstetrical errors have at least two plaintiffs: the mother and the infant

   d. Although negligence and malpractice are the most common claims for this practice setting, the nature of the care provided and the type of procedures used are also subject to intentional torts and civil rights violations

   e. Professional standards of care established for obstetrical nursing have a significant impact on the liability incurred by the practicing nurse

   f. The ANA defines obstetrical nursing as a specialty that emphasizes the health needs of children and the health needs of women, parents, and families throughout their reproductive years

   g. *Nurse generalists* who work in the obstetrical unit have a generic nursing preparation, with additional training in the specialized area of maternal-child health nursing

   h. *Maternal-child specialists* who work in the obstetrical unit have a master's degree and can provide expert nursing care for women throughout childbearing

2. Sources of legal action

   a. Because the courts recognize that a legal duty is owed to the unborn, an obstetrical nurse can be charged with violating the rights of a fetus as well as those of the mother

   b. An obstetrical nurse may be held liable for negligence through participation in negligent transfusion of incompatible blood, especially in relation to Rh factor incompatibility; failure to attend to or monitor the mother or the fetus during labor and delivery; failure to recognize labor symptoms and to provide adequate support and care; failure to monitor contractions and fetal heart rate, particularly in obstetrical units that have internal monitoring capabilities; and failure to recognize high-risk labor patients who show signs of preeclampsia or other labor complications that demand prompt action for a safe delivery

    c. Parents can file a *wrongful birth* lawsuit if a nurse failed to advise them of contraceptive methods or the methods' potential for failure, potential genetic defects, the availability of amniocentesis to detect defects, or abortion to prevent birth of a defective child

    d. A child with a genetic defect can file a *wrongful life* lawsuit if a nurse failed to inform the parents of amniocentesis and the option of abortion

    e. A nurse's failure to provide adequate genetic counseling and prenatal testing when the mother has a history of Down's syndrome can also result in a wrongful birth or wrongful life lawsuit

    f. Failure to warn parents of the risks of diagnostic tests—and the consequences of refusing such tests—can be the basis of legal actions against obstetrical nurses if the failure contributes to maternal or fetal injury

    g. *Abandonment*—the unilateral severance of a professional relationship with a patient without adequate notice and while the patient still needs attention—can occur at any time during the patient's hospitalization but usually is the basis of a lawsuit when the patient was in active labor

    h. Failure to exercise independent judgment, such as carrying out medical orders that the nurse knows will harm the patient, is becoming more common as a liability claim

    i. Failure to ensure that a patient has given informed consent for various procedures or treatments—including physical examinations, administration of a potent medication, type of delivery method, sterilization, and postdelivery surgical procedures—can result in an unintentional tort claim of malpractice and an intentional tort claim of assault and battery

    j. Failure to obtain informed consent for a sterilization procedure can also be ruled a civil rights violation, especially if the patient is incompetent or mentally retarded or if the sterilization is ordered by the state

    k. Other common sources of malpractice suits filed against obstetrical nurses include failure to attend to the infant in distress, failure to monitor equipment, use of defective equipment, failure to monitor oxygen levels, and failure to recognize and report newborn jaundice during the immediate postnatal period

3. Implications for nurses

    a. To practice obstetrical nursing competently, a nurse must be able to recognize the major signs and symptoms of the leading causes of maternal and infant death and must keep abreast of knowledge in their prevention, detection, and treatment

    b. Obstetrical nurses can minimize their risk of liability by meeting the professional standards of care established for this practice setting

    c. Nurses should take special care to instruct patients about the reasons for genetic screening tests and the potential consequences of refusing the tests

   d. Proper monitoring of a patient requires careful observation and documentation throughout pregnancy, including labor and delivery
   e. Nurses must be familiar with the signs and symptoms of high-risk delivery and respond appropriately to potential complications
   f. A nurse can countersue a hospital if an unfavorable judgment against the nurse was based on defective equipment used at the time of a patient's injury
   g. If an obstetrical nurse is unfamiliar with a procedure or the required care for a patient, the nurse should decline the assignment and the supervisor should delegate it to another nurse
   h. Obstetrical nurses should become involved in their own practice standards by establishing and participating in policy and procedure committees and ethics committees

**F. Operating room and recovery room**
   1. General information
      a. The legal duty of an operating room nurse is the same as that of any other nurse: to provide reasonable and prudent patient care so as not to cause injury
      b. Operating room nurses practice in various locations, including traditional operating rooms, specialized procedure rooms, 1-day surgery areas, and outpatient surgical facilities
      c. The nature of surgery involves intrusive and potentially destructive actions by health care providers
      d. Because of anesthesia or heavy sedation, patients in the operating room cannot protect themselves from injury
      e. A sedated, unconscious patient cannot feel pain or take actions to prevent further infliction of injury
      f. Other than the critical care unit, the operating room usually has the newest, most sophisticated technological equipment, including monitors, lasers, and computers
      g. Because of the danger inherent in surgery and the technically sophisticated equipment and procedures used, operating room nursing standards place major emphasis on patient safety
      h. Legal doctrines traditionally associated with operating room injuries include the captain of the ship doctrine, the borrowed servant doctrine, and *res ipsa loquitur*
      i. According to the captain of the ship doctrine, a surgeon has complete authority in the operating room, is responsible to the patient for all acts performed by all personnel, and thus accepts all liability; this doctrine is almost never used today
      j. According to the borrowed servant doctrine, operating room nurses are employees of the hospital but under the direction of the surgeon; therefore, liability for negligence is shared among the nurse, the hospital, and the surgeon

k.  According to the doctrine of *res ipsa loquitur* ("the thing speaks for itself"), the burden of proof shifts from the patient (plaintiff) to the defendant, who must prove that negligence did not occur; injuries to anesthetized patients usually result from surgical negligence

l.  Because *res ipsa loquitur* is easily established when personal injury occurs in the operating room, this doctrine is applied more frequently to operating room incidents than to incidents in any other practice setting

2.  Sources of legal action

a.  Failure to ensure that a patient has given an informed consent can result in illegal, fraudulent, or contraindicated surgery

b.  Leaving a foreign object inside a patient—the most common type of negligence charge brought against an operating room nurse—falls under the *res ipsa loquitur* doctrine; furthermore, because a patient may not discover for some time that a surgical instrument or sponge had been left inside him during surgery, the courts usually permit liberal variations in the statute of limitations

c.  Abandonment (severing the nurse-patient relationship without the patient's consent) can be classified as breach of contract, an intentional tort, or professional negligence, any of which is difficult for an operating room nurse to defend because an anesthetized patient cannot legally consent to anything

d.  Working outside the scope of nursing practice (a violation of the nurse practice act) can present legal and financial problems for an operating room nurse who functions as a surgeon's first assistant (a role ordinarily performed by another physician); most malpractice insurance policies consider this role as outside the nurse's scope of practice and exclude coverage when a nurse serves in this capacity

e.  Failure to monitor a patient recovering from anesthesia is a common complaint in lawsuits against recovery room nurses

f.  Prematurely discharging a patient from the recovery room before he is fully awake or failing to detect hypoxia or lethal cardiac arrhythmias in a recovering patient can result in a wrongful death lawsuit against a recovery room nurse

g.  Using defective equipment and failing to position a patient properly can result in burns and peroneal nerve paralysis, two of the most common injuries associated with the operating room and recovery room

3.  Implications for nurses

a.  Emphasizing patient safety is the best legal protection for operating room and recovery room nurses

b.  Nurses who work in these practice settings should take special care to prevent ulnar or peroneal nerve paralysis from improper positioning and burns from defective equipment

    c. Although obtaining an informed consent is the surgeon's responsibility, an operating room nurse has a duty to ensure that the informed consent has been obtained; thus, if a surgeon is about to perform or is performing a procedure to which a patient did not consent, the nurse has an obligation to make this fact known to the surgeon and to document it in the record

    d. Operating room and recovery room nurses should insist that their hospital have a written policy that outlines the steps to take when a patient arrives in the operating room without a valid informed consent

    e. To prevent a foreign object from being left in a patient, operating room nurses must pay strict attention and carefully count surgical instruments, sponges, and other equipment used during surgery

    f. An operating room or recovery room nurse should not leave a patient unattended, even for a short time, unless the patient's safety demands it

    g. Nurses who work as first surgical assistants are undertaking activities of another profession, are held to the standards of care for that profession, and will most likely lose the protection of their own license

    h. Because of the surgical patient's particular vulnerability to injury, operating room and recovery room nurses should be involved in the development of safety procedures, policies, and precautions

    i. Complete and accurate charting can help operating room and recovery room nurses prove that they were not negligent; checklists and graphic charts can lessen the amount of time needed for charting while helping nurses document safety measures taken to prevent injury

## G. Medical-surgical unit

1. General information
   a. According to the ANA, medical-surgical nursing is "the nursing care of individuals who have a known or predicted physiological alteration"
   b. Most nurses employed by hospitals work in medical-surgical units
   c. Various practice settings—including primary, acute, and long-term care—fall under the umbrella of medical-surgical nursing
2. Sources of legal action
   a. A medical-surgical nurse can be charged with negligence as a result of various actions or inactions that harm a patient, such as failing to follow preapproved standing orders (which require a certain nursing action in a certain situation); failing to protect a patient from a dangerous condition (such as infection or falls); violating one or more of the five "rights" of medication administration (right drug, right dose, right patient, right time, and right route); failing to monitor I.V. lines carefully (which can lead to infiltration, subsequent tissue damage, and loss of a limb); failing to prevent or recognize equipment malfunctioning (which can result in burns or electrical injury); failing to monitor a patient, report his condition, or take appropriate action; or agreeing to work in understaffed conditions or with unqualified personnel

b.  Another form of negligence — failure to attend to the patient — is similar to abandonment in that both involve a nurse who leaves a patient alone when the patient needs close attention, usually when he is unconscious, delirious, heavily medicated, or subject to spells of dizziness or weakness

c.  Failure to exercise independent judgment — a charge being brought with greater frequency against medical-surgical nurses — can result if a nurse follows a physician's order that is inappropriate, not in accordance with accepted practice, or clearly harmful to the patient

d.  Failure to recognize and report substandard treatment regarding medication or other treatment orders renders both the nurse and the physician liable for legal action

3.  Implications for nurses

a.  Careful recording and documenting of observations and nursing actions can help nurses prove that negligence did not occur

b.  Medical-surgical nurses must have a basic knowledge and understanding of any drug administered, including acceptable dose, route, side effects, and interactions

c.  Inappropriate or harmful care by a physician must be brought to the attention of the physician, the hospital administration, or both

d.  Nurses need to remember that the nurse-patient relationship is one of patient advocacy, whereby the nurse protects a dependent patient from injury and danger

e.  Accepting responsibility to work with patients renders nurses accountable for the care they provide — and liable for any harm that may arise from accepting the responsibility, including the increased liabilities involved when working in understaffed conditions or with unqualified personnel

## H.  Out-of-hospital practice settings

1.  General information

a.  Many nurses work outside the hospital as public health nurses, school nurses, or occupational health nurses

b.  All three practice settings share the common elements of independence of practice, expanded practice role, and state and federal enforcement of health care laws

c.  Nurses in these settings play a dual role, promoting and preserving the health of specific populations while treating various health problems that arise

d.  Legal actions against nurses in out-of-hospital practice settings have been minimal compared to those involving the recovery room, critical care unit, and obstetrical unit

e.  In many jurisdictions, public health nurses, school nurses, and occupational health nurses are protected from liability by various state legal exemptions

2. Sources of legal action
   a. Failure to educate a patient sufficiently about medications or to assess his response to medication therapy is a particular concern in the public health setting, where powerful and potentially dangerous medications are used to treat tuberculosis and other infectious diseases
   b. Failure to report suspected child abuse or to respond to a report of child abuse can result in negligence charges against public health nurses and school nurses
   c. Lack of informed consent can pose a legal problem for a school nurse because of the patient's age
   d. Failure to manage accidents adequately and provide first aid can result in successful litigation against school nurses and occupational health nurses
   e. Failure of an occupational health nurse to report an employer who violates public health laws is a violation of state or federal occupational safety and health laws
   f. Failure to assess an injury appropriately and seek emergency care can be the source of a negligence suit against a nurse in any of these practice settings
   g. A nurse in any out-of-hospital setting who knowingly, arbitrarily, and carelessly refrains from performing a duty imposed by law can be charged with second-degree official misconduct
3. Implications for nurses
   a. Nurses must ensure that each patient has given an informed consent for all treatments and medications and must adequately warn the patient of potential side effects of medications
   b. Nurses who work outside the hospital setting are expected to know and enforce public health laws
   c. Medication administration by school nurses should be governed by a policy that requires permission from the parents and physician
   d. School nurses and occupational health nurses must know when to refer an accident victim for further treatment
   e. Nurses in all three practice settings should periodically review the standing orders for medications and emergencies and update the orders as needed
   f. Nurses should keep up-to-date on all federal and state laws that pertain to their practice
   g. Although nurses who work outside the hospital have traditionally avoided the large number of lawsuits plaguing their hospital-based colleagues, new liability situations will probably arise if technological changes and the current trend toward litigation continue

## Points to Remember

Nurses are increasingly being named as defendants or codefendants in malpractice lawsuits.

Nurses whose practice settings involve sophisticated technology, invasive procedures, or increased bedside time with a patient are at a high risk of liability for negligence.

Medication errors, abandonment, failure to assess the patient's condition and respond appropriately, and lack of informed consent are fertile grounds for malpractice suits in all practice settings.

Failure to exercise independent judgment (carrying out medical orders that are inappropriate or clearly harmful to a patient) is a charge being brought against nurses with increasing frequency.

## Glossary

**Abandonment**—unilateral severance of a professional relationship with a patient without adequate notice and while the need for medical or nursing care still exists

**Breach of care**—failure to provide safe and proper care, whether or not the patient was injured

**Floating**—temporary assignment of a nurse who normally works on one unit to work on another unit, usually to fill a staff shortage

**Good Samaritan laws**—laws that protect an individual from liability for care provided in a true emergency; these laws, based on the concept of implied consent, are intended to encourage those with advanced knowledge in health care, such as doctors and nurses, to help in emergencies without fear of being sued

**True emergency**—situation in which a patient faces death or serious bodily injury unless immediate medical or nursing care is rendered

**Wrongful treatment**—medical or nursing intervention that violates a patient's right to self-determination or the family's wishes

# Avoiding Legal Jeopardy

## Learning Objectives

After studying this section, the reader should be able to:

● Identify personality traits and behaviors of patients who are likely to file lawsuits and of nurses who are likely to be named as defendants.

● List the ways in which nurses can protect themselves from legal action.

● Differentiate among the three types of professional liability insurance.

● Name the provisions commonly found in professional liability insurance policies.

● Discuss the implications of professional liability insurance for nurses and nursing practice.

## XI. Avoiding Legal Jeopardy

### A. Introduction
1. Although legal jeopardy looms menacingly over a nurse's every action, only 1 of every 1,000 nurses is charged with malpractice, and fewer still are convicted of malpractice or other legal infractions
2. Preventing situations that produce legal jeopardy is easier than dealing with the consequences after an incident occurs
3. Patients who are more likely to file lawsuits against nurses share certain personality traits and behaviors, and nurses who are more likely to be named as defendants also have certain characteristics in common

### B. Patients who file lawsuits
1. Patients who tend to file lawsuits against nurses display certain behaviors not typical of other patients, although not all persons displaying these behaviors file a lawsuit
2. A nurse who provides professional and competent care to such patients will lessen their tendency to sue
3. A patient who is more likely to file a lawsuit is one who:
   a. Persistently criticizes all aspects of the nursing care provided
   b. Purposefully does not follow the plan of care
   c. Overreacts to any perceived slight or negative comment about him, real or imagined
   d. Unjustifiably depends on nurses for all aspects of care, refusing to accept any responsibility for his own care
   e. Openly expresses hostility to nurses and other health care personnel
   f. Projects his anxiety, fear, or anger onto the nursing staff, attributing blame for all negative events to the health care providers
   g. Has filed lawsuits previously

### C. Nurses who are named as defendants
1. Nurses who are more likely to be named as defendants in a lawsuit display certain behaviors not typical of other nurses
2. A nurse who can change these behaviors will reduce the risk of liability
3. A nurse who is more likely to be named as a defendant is one who:
   a. Is insensitive to the patient's complaints or does not take them seriously
   b. Does not identify and meet the patient's emotional and physical needs
   c. Does not realize the limits of nursing skills and personal competency
   d. Lacks sufficient education for the tasks and responsibilities associated with a specific practice setting
   e. Displays an authoritarian and inflexible attitude when providing care
   f. Inappropriately delegates responsibilities to subordinates

## D. Self-protection from lawsuits

1. Improving individual nursing competency and collaborating with coworkers to improve the quality of care provided in their practice setting will significantly reduce a nurse's risk of liability

2. Nurses can help ensure safe, ethical, and competent nursing practice — and therefore greatly reduce the possibility of legal entanglements — by following these guidelines:

   a. Identify personal nursing strengths and weaknesses, and then take steps to work on the areas that need improvement

   b. Avoid accepting responsibilities or assignments for which one's education and training are insufficient

   c. Keep telephone orders to a minimum, always repeat the order to the physician, and obtain the physician's countersignature on all orders, written or verbal, within 24 hours

   d. Don't carry out an order or instruction that raises doubts; try to obtain clarification or verification of the order

   e. Carefully observe the patient for adverse effects from any medication or treatment, and report them immediately

   f. Know and follow institutional policies and procedures, and actively participate in revising old ones and developing new ones when needed

   g. If violating a policy or procedure is necessary for the patient's well-being, carefully document the circumstances, the reasons for doing so, and the outcome

   h. Document — accurately, completely, and legibly in nurse's notes — all observations, decisions, actions, and outcomes that result from decisions or actions; be especially thorough if a patient's behavior suggests he would be likely to file a lawsuit

   i. Be realistic and objective when documenting a patient's progress; avoid overly optimistic or overly pessimistic statements

   j. Try not to become defensive with a hostile patient; this only widens the barrier between patient and nurse

   k. Avoid making any statement that could be perceived by the patient as an admission of fault or error

   l. Avoid criticizing other nurses, other health care practitioners, or the care they provide

   m. Provide clear, specific instructions to the patient, preferably in writing

   n. Maintain strict confidentiality of all patient communications and medical information

   o. Use incident reports to identify and report any accidents, errors, or injuries to a patient; instead of placing incident reports in the patient's chart, give them directly to the institution's risk manager

   p. Exercise great care as a supervisor when delegating duties because a supervisor can be held responsible for errors committed by subordinates

  q. Inspect all equipment and machinery regularly, and be sure that subordinates use them competently and safely

  r. Report incompetent health care personnel to superiors through the institutional chain of command

  s. Be tactful and professional when working with patients and their families; try to establish a productive rapport with them so they see the nurse as a patient advocate in the health care system

  t. Don't discuss with the patient or visitors which members of the health care team are covered by malpractice insurance

  u. Be sure to carry sufficient malpractice insurance

**E. Malpractice insurance**

 1. General information

  a. In malpractice insurance, or professional liability insurance, the insurer agrees to provide monetary compensation coverage to a professsional for acts of professional negligence

  b. An uninsured or underinsured nurse feels that the risk of being sued and found guilty is not sufficient to justify the premium price of the insurance and instead assumes personal responsibility for financial damages awarded to a patient; the money can be paid from the nurse's personal assets, liens placed on property, or garnishment of current and future earnings

  c. All professional liability insurance policies contain an insuring agreement (which promises that the insurer will provide legal counsel to defend against lawsuits and pay for awards against the nurse up to specified limits), a statement of the conditions of the contract (including obligations of the insured and the insurer), exclusionary clauses (which specify certain acts not covered by the policy), and "other insurance" clauses (which address payment obligations when a nurse is covered by more than one insurance policy, such as the institution's policy and the nurse's personal liability policy)

  d. "Other insurance" clauses are of three types (pro rata, in excess, and escape), and they may or may not conflict

  e. The *pro rata* clause states that two or more policies in effect at the same time will pay any claims in accordance with a proportion established in the individual policies

  f. The *in excess* clause states that the primary policy will pay all fees and damages up to its limits, at which point the second policy will pay any additional fees or damages up to its limits

  g. The *escape clause* relieves an insurance company of all liability for fees or damages if another insurance policy is in effect at the same time; in effect, the clause states that the other policy is responsible for all liability

2. Types of malpractice policies
   a. An *individual professional liability policy* covers individual health care providers, such as nurses; the policy is issued in the name of the provider for a specified time and covers specific types of activities
   b. An *institutional liability policy* covers employees, such as nurses, acting within the scope of their employment; the policy can be issued to hospitals, nursing homes, home health care agencies, and psychiatric hospitals
   c. A *commercial liability policy* covers partnerships, corporations, professional service organizations, and other businesses; the policy may or may not cover nurses, depending on their relationship to the business as partners, officers, or agents
3. Policy provisions
   a. All professional liability insurance policies have provisions that specify the identity of the insured and the duration of coverage
   b. *Claims-made policies* cover claims reported during the policy period for incidents occurring either before or during the policy period but do not cover claims made after the policy has been terminated
   c. *Occurrence policies* cover claims for incidents that occur during the policy period, including claims filed after the policy has terminated
   d. Policy limits—the maximum dollar amount available for coverage—usually are expressed as a proportion, such as $X/$Y, where X is the maximum amount available to settle one claim and Y is the maximum amount available to settle all claims during the policy period (usually 1 year)
   e. Although most professional liability insurers accept their duty to defend the insured in any legal action, the duty must be specified in the policy, usually a statement in which the insurer promises to provide a competent attorney or employ an attorney on the insured's behalf
   f. Most policies also specify claim settlement procedures (including whether or not the insured's consent is needed for the insurer to settle a claim), the insurer's obligation to cover the insured in cases of appeal (if not in writing, the obligation usually is assumed), the right of either party to cancel a policy (usually including specific grounds for cancellation, a 30-day notification period, and the right not to renew the policy), and the right of indemnification (which, in an institutional policy, allows the insurer to seek recovery from the insured's employee when negligence was solely the employee's responsibility)
   g. The insurance application is a legal document, and any false information provided by the insured may void the policy
   h. The insured has an obligation to notify the insurer as soon as possible if the insured is threatened with a lawsuit by any patient or family member, receives a letter from a patient's attorney, is served with legal papers, or becomes aware that a patient has been injured or harmed by medication administered or treatment given by the insured

      i. The insured has a duty to cooperate with the insurer and offer whatever help is required in defending against the claim, including truthful disclosure of all facts and avoidance of any admission of fault

4. Policy limitations
    a. Professional liability coverage is limited to the acts and practice settings specified in the policy
    b. Coverage does not extend to criminal acts
    c. Coverage may not extend to intentional torts if intent to do harm is proved
    d. Coverage does not extend to medical or nursing actions that the insured has promised or guaranteed will be successful
    e. Coverage does not extend to acts outside the scope of practice or licensure
    f. Coverage may or may not extend to punitive damages (additional money awarded to the victim over and above the actual damages), depending on the policy

5. Implications for nurses
    a. Insurance protection must be adequate — under one's personal liability insurance policy or the employer's institutional policy — for all aspects of nursing practice
    b. The policy should cover professional services provided in a particular care setting; an occurrence policy provides more coverage than a claims-made policy
    c. A nurse involved in nursing administration, education, research, or advanced or nontraditional nursing practice should use special precaution in selecting a policy because routine policies may not cover these activities
    d. A nurse covered by more than one policy should be alert for "other insurance" clauses in a policy and avoid those with an escape clause for liability
    e. Insurance policies issued to physicians or groups of physicians who employ nurses usually cover a nurse only when the policy identifies the nurse by name
    f. After selecting a policy that ensures adequate coverage, the nurse should stay with the same policy and insurer, if possible, to avoid potential lapses in coverage that could occur when changing insurers
    g. The nurse should uphold all obligations specified in the policy; failure to do so may void the policy and cause personal liability for any damages
    h. Willful wrongdoing constitutes bad faith on the part of the insured, which renders the policy null and void and may lead to a breach of contract lawsuit
    i. A nurse who is threatened with a lawsuit or is under any other circumstances specified in the policy must notify the insurer as soon as possible

j.  The nurse must disclose all facts truthfully and completely to the insurer

k.  An insurer is relieved of all liability if a nurse makes promises to a patient about the results of any treatment

l.  The activities a nurse performs should be within the scope of nursing practice established by the nurse practice act

m.  A careful nurse becomes involved in professional nurses' association activities that deal with insurance and scope of practice issues

## Points to Remember

Patients who are likely to file lawsuits and nurses who are likely to be named as defendants display certain behavioral characteristics that make them easy to identify.

Safe, ethical, and competent nursing practice is the best protection against legal jeopardy.

Careful and thorough documentation of nursing care provided is important in defending a nurse's judgments, decisions, and actions.

An uninsured or underinsured nurse presumes that the risk of being sued and found guilty is insufficient to justify the premium price of the insurance; in assuming personal responsibility for financial damages awarded to a patient, the nurse risks losing personal assets, property, and wages.

An occurrence policy provides more coverage than a claims-made policy because it protects the insured for incidents that occurred during the policy period but were not reported until after the policy had expired

## Glossary

**Bad faith** — willful, fraudulent wrongdoing that usually renders a contract null and void and that could expose an insured party to a breach of contract lawsuit

**Garnishment** — court seizure of a defendant's wages or property to pay fines or damages awarded to a plaintiff

**Indemnification** — right of an employer's insurer to seek reimbursement from an employee for damages paid as a result of the employee's negligence

# Appendices

## Appendix A

### LIVING WILL

Most states and the District of Columbia have passed laws that allow a person to instruct family and health care professionals about medical steps he wants taken or not taken if he becomes terminally ill. Usually, a living will authorizes the attending physician to withhold or discontinue life-saving procedures (see sample below).

---

**LIVING WILL**
DECLARATION
SAMPLE*

Declaration made this _____day of _____ 199 _____

I, _____, being of sound mind, willfully and voluntarily make known my desires that my dying shall not be artificially prolonged under the circumstances set forth below, and do declare:

If at any time I should have an incurable injury, disease, or illness certified to be a terminal condition by two (2) physicians who have personally examined me, one of whom shall be my attending physician, and the physicians have determined that my death will occur whether or not life-sustaining procedures are utilized and where the application of life-sustaining procedures would serve only to artificially prolong the dying process, I direct that such procedures be withheld or withdrawn, and that I be permitted to die naturally with only the administration of medication or the performance of any medical procedure deemed necessary to provide me with comfort or care or to alleviate pain.

In the absence of my ability to give directions regarding the use of such life-sustaining procedures, it is my intention that this declaration shall be honored by my family and physician(s) as the final expression of my legal right to refuse medical or surgical treatment and accept the consequences from such refusal.

I understand the full import of this declaration and I am emotionally and mentally competent to make this declaration.

Signed _____

Address _____

I believe the declarant to be of sound mind. I did not sign the declarant's signature above for or at the direction of the declarant. I am at least 18 years of age and am not related to the declarant by blood or marriage, entitled to any portion of the estate of the declarant according to the laws of intestate succession of the _____ or under any will of the declarant or codicil thereto, or directly financially responsible for declarant's medical care. I am not the declarant's attending physician, an employee of the attending physician, or an employee of the health facility in which the declarant is a patient.

Witness _____

Address _____

Witness _____

Address _____

ss.:

**LIVING WILL** continued

Before me, the undersigned authority, on this _____ day of _____, 199___, personally appeared _____, _____, and _____, known to me to be the Declarant and the witnesses, respectively, whose names are signed to the foregoing instrument, and who, in the presence of each other, did subscribe their names to the attached Declaration (Living Will) on this date, and that said Declarant at the time of execution of said Declaration was over the age of eighteen (18) years and of sound mind.

[Seal]
My commission expires:

_____
Notary Public

*Check requirements of individual state statute.*

Sample form is reprinted from *Modern Maturity* (June/July, 1988), p. 33, with permission of the American Association of Retired Persons. Form originally appeared in the AARP's *A Matter of Choice,* prepared for the U.S. Senate Special Committee on Aging.

## Appendix B

### DURABLE POWER OF ATTORNEY

To ensure that a person's living will is carried out, he may execute a durable power of attorney like the one shown here. Unlike a living will, a durable power of attorney form provides blank lines for the person to specify his wishes about life-support measures and to list limitations or provisions if appropriate.

---

### DURABLE POWER OF ATTORNEY
#### FOR HEALTH CARE
##### SAMPLE*

I, _____
hereby appoint: _____
name _____
home address _____
home telephone number _____
work telephone number _____
as my agent to make health care decisions for me if and when I am unable to make my own health care decisions. This gives my agent the power to consent to giving, withholding, or stopping any health care, treatment, service, or diagnostic procedure. My agent also has the authority to talk with health care personnel, get information, and sign forms necessary to carry out those decisions.

If the person named as my agent is not available or is unable to act as my agent, then I appoint the following person(s) to serve in the order listed below:

**1.** name _____
home address _____
home telephone number _____
work telephone number _____

**2.** name _____
home address _____
home telephone number _____
work telephone number _____

By this document I intend to create a power of attorney for health care which shall take effect upon my incapacity to make my own health care decisions and shall continue during that incapacity.

My agent shall make health care decisions as I direct below or as I make known to him or her in some other way.

(a) Statement of desires concerning life-prolonging care, treatment, services, and procedures:

_____
_____
_____
_____

(b) Special provisions and limitations:
_____
_____
_____
_____
_____
_____
_____

**By signing here I indicate that I understand the purpose and effect of this document.**

I sign my name to this form on

_____
(date)

My current home address:
_____
_____
_____
(You sign here)

## DURABLE POWER OF ATTORNEY continued

### WITNESSES

I declare that the person who signed or acknowledged this document is personally known to me, that he/she signed or acknowledged this durable power of attorney in my presence, and that he/she appears to be of sound mind and under no duress, fraud, or undue influence. I am not the person appointed as agent by this document, nor am I the patient's health care provider, or an employee of the patient's health care provider.

**First Witness**
Signature: _____
Home Address: _____
Print Name: _____
Date: _____

**Second Witness**
Signature: _____
Home Address: _____
Print Name: _____
Date: _____
(At least one of the above witnesses must also sign the following declaration.)

I further declare that I am not related to the patient by blood, marriage, or adoption, and, to the best of my knowledge, I am not entitled to any part of his/her estate under a will now existing or by operation of law.

Signature: _____

Signature: _____

I further declare that I am not related to the patient by blood, marriage, or adoption, and, to the best of my knowledge, I am not entitled to any part of his/her estate under a will now existing or by operation of law.

Signature: _____

Signature: _____

*Check requirements of individual state statute.*

Sample form is reprinted from *Modern Maturity* (June/July, 1988), p. 88, with permission of the American Association of Retired Persons. Form originally appeared in the AARP's *A Matter of Choice,* prepared for the U.S. Senate Special Committee on Aging.

## Appendix C

### UNIFORM ANATOMICAL GIFT ACT

All 50 states have adopted the Uniform Anatomical Gift Act, which provides two ways to donate organs:

• In Canada and the United States, any person 18 or older may indicate his desire to become an organ donor by signing a uniform donor card in the presence of two witnesses (see sample below). In many states, this intent is recorded on the back of a driver's license. Although the person's signature legally indicates his wish to be a donor, his next-of-kin must still sign a donation consent form when he dies.

• A family member may authorize donation of a decedent's organs by signing a donation consent form. If death occurs within 24 hours of admission to a hospital or results from an accident, homicide, or other unnatural cause, a medical examiner must also consent to the organ donation.

Of course, before any donation can occur, death must be legally established.

---

**UNIFORM DONOR CARD**

x _____
*Print or type name of donor*

In the hope that I may help others, I hereby make this anatomical gift, if medically acceptable, to take effect upon my death. The words and marks below indicate my desires.

I give: (a) _____ any needed organs or parts
(b) _____ only the following organs or parts

_____
*Specify the organ(s) or part(s)*
for the purposes of transplantation, therapy, medical research, or education; (c) _____ my body for anatomical study if needed.

Limitations or special wishes, if any: _____

**FRONT**

---

Signed by the donor and the following two witnesses in the presence of each other.

_____          _____
Signature of donor                       Date of birth of donor

_____          _____
Date signed                                 City and State

_____          _____
Witness                                      Witness

This is a legal document under the Uniform Anatomical Gift Act or similar laws. For further information consult your physician or local National Kidney Foundation Office.
☐ Yes, I have discussed my wishes with my family.

**BACK**

---

# Appendix D

## UNITED STATES BOARDS OF NURSING

**ALABAMA**
**State Board of Nursing**
500 East Blvd., Suite 203
Montgomery, AL 36117

**ALASKA**
**Board of Nursing Licensing**
Dept. of Commerce and Economic
Development
Pouch D
Juneau, AK 99811

**Board of Nursing**
142 E. 3rd Ave.
Anchorage, AK 99501

**ARIZONA**
**State Board of Nursing**
1645 W. Jefferson, Rm. 254
Phoenix, AZ 85007

**ARKANSAS**
**State Board of Nursing**
4120 W. Markham, Suite 308
Little Rock, AR 77205

**CALIFORNIA**
**Board of Registered Nursing**
1020 N. St.
Sacramento, CA 95814

**COLORADO**
**State Board of Nursing**
1525 Sherman St.
Denver, CO 80203

**CONNECTICUT**
**Board of Examiners for Nursing**
79 Elm St.
Hartford, CT 06106

**DELAWARE**
**Board of Nursing**
Margaret O'Neill Bldg.
Federal & Court Sts.
Dover, DE 19901

**DISTRICT OF COLUMBIA**
**Registered Nurses Examining Board**
614 H St., NW
Washington, DC 20001

**FLORIDA**
**Board of Nursing**
111 E. Coastline Dr.
Jacksonville, FL 32202

**GEORGIA**
**Board of Nursing**
166 Pryor St., SW
Atlanta, GA 30303

**HAWAII**
**Board of Nursing**
P.O. Box 3469
Honolulu, HI 96801

**IDAHO**
**State Board of Nursing**
Hall of Mirrors
700 W. State, 2nd Fl.
Boise, ID 83720

**ILLINOIS**
**Department of Registration & Education**
Nurse Section
320 W. Washington St.
Springfield, IL 62786

**INDIANA**
**State Board of Nurses Registration and**
**Nursing Education**
964 N. Pennsylvania
Indianapolis, IN 46204

**IOWA**
**Board of Nursing**
1223 E. Court
Des Moines, IA 50319

**KANSAS**
**State Board of Nursing**
P.O. Box 1098
503 Kansas Ave.
Topeka, KS 66601

**KENTUCKY**
**Board of Nursing Education and Nurse**
**Registration**
4010 Dupont Circle
Louisville, KY 40207

continued

## UNITED STATES BOARDS OF NURSING continued

**LOUISIANA**
**State Board of Nursing**
150 Baronne St.
New Orleans, LA 70112

**MAINE**
**State Board of Nursing**
295 Water St.
Augusta, ME 04330

**MARYLAND**
**Board of Examiners of Nurses**
201 W. Preston St.
Baltimore, MD 21201

**MASSACHUSETTS**
**Board of Registration in Nursing**
100 Cambridge St., Rm. 1509
Boston, MA 02202

**MICHIGAN**
**Board of Nursing**
P.O. Box 30018
905 Southland
Lansing, MI 48909

**MINNESOTA**
**Board of Nursing**
717 Delaware St., SE
Minneapolis, MN 55414

**MISSISSIPPI**
**Board of Nursing**
135 Bounds St., Suite 101
Jackson, MS 39206

**MISSOURI**
3523 N. Ten Mile Dr.
Box 656
Jefferson City, MO 65102-0656

**MONTANA**
**Board of Nursing**
Dept. of Commerce
1424 9th Ave.
Helena, MT 59620

**NEBRASKA**
**State Board of Nursing**
Box 95065
State House Station
Lincoln, NE 68509

**NEVADA**
**Board of Nursing**
1135 Terminal Way
Reno, NV 89502

**NEW HAMPSHIRE**
**Board of Nursing Education and Nurse Registration**
105 Loudon Rd.
Concord, NH 03301

**NEW JERSEY**
**Board of Nursing**
1100 Raymond Blvd.
Newark, NJ 07102

**NEW MEXICO**
**Board of Nursing**
5301 Central NE
Albuquerque, NM 87108

**NEW YORK**
**Board for Nursing**
State Education Department
Cultural Education Center
Albany, NY 12230

**NORTH CAROLINA**
**Board of Nursing**
Box 2129
Raleigh, NC 27602

**NORTH DAKOTA**
**Board of Nursing**
418 E. Rosser Ave.
Bismarck, ND 58501

**OHIO**
**Board of Nursing Education and Nurse Registration**
65 S. Front St.
Columbus, OH 43215

## UNITED STATES BOARDS OF NURSING continued

**OKLAHOMA**
**Board of Nurse Registration and**
**Nursing Education**
4001 N. Lincoln Blvd., Suite 400
Oklahoma City, OK 73105

**OREGON**
**Board of Nursing**
1400 SW 5th Ave.
Portland, OR 97201

**PENNSYLVANIA**
**State Board of Nurse Examiners**
Box 2649
Harrisburg, PA 17120

**RHODE ISLAND**
**Board of Nurse Registration and**
**Nursing Education**
Cannon Health Building
75 Davis St.
Providence, RI 02908

**SOUTH CAROLINA**
**Board of Nursing**
1777 St. Julian Place, Suite 102
Columbia, SC 29204

**SOUTH DAKOTA**
**Board of Nursing**
304 S. Phillips Ave.
Sioux Falls, SD 57102

**TENNESSEE**
**Board of Nursing**
TDPH State Office Bldg.
Ben Allen Rd.
Nashville, TN 37216

**TEXAS**
**Board of Nurse Examiners**
1300 E. Anderson Lane, Bldg. C
Austin, TX 78752

**UTAH**
**Division of Registration Board of**
**Nursing**
Heber M. Wells Bldg.
160 E. 300 South
P.O. Box 5802
Salt Lake City, UT 84110

**VERMONT**
**Board of Nursing**
Pavilion Office Bldg.
109 State St.
Montpelier, VT 05602

**VIRGINIA**
**Board of Nursing**
517 W. Grace St.
P.O. Box 27708
Richmond, VA 23261

**WASHINGTON**
**Board of Nursing**
Box 9649
Olympia, WA 98504

**WEST VIRGINIA**
**Board of Nurse Examiners**
Embleton Bldg.
922 Quarrier St.
Charleston, WV 25301

**WISCONSIN**
**Board of Nursing**
P.O. Box 8936
Madison, WI 53708

**WYOMING**
**Board of Nursing**
2223 Warren Ave.
Cheyenne, WY 82002

# Appendix E

## INTERPRETING LEGAL CITATIONS

To look up a law (statute or regulation) or court case, go to the county courthouse law library or local law school library with legal citation in hand. For an overview or summary of a law or court case, look up the citation in a standard legal reference, such as a legal encyclopedia (*Corpus Juris Secundum*) or a legal text (*Restatements of Law*).

To locate a complete text of the law or case, you must first have a full citation, such as the ones shown here.

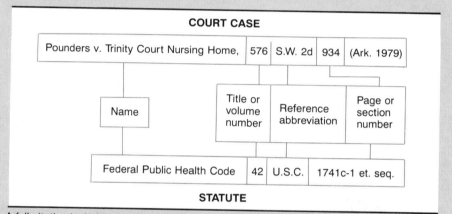

**COURT CASE**

Pounders v. Trinity Court Nursing Home, | 576 | S.W. 2d | 934 | (Ark. 1979)

Name

Title or volume number — Reference abbreviation — Page or section number

Federal Public Health Code | 42 | U.S.C. | 1741c-1 et. seq.

**STATUTE**

A full citation includes the name of the law or court case and a series of identifying numbers and letters. If some or all of the identifying numbers and letters are missing, look up the law or case number in the index of one of the legal references listed on pages 111 and 112.

The letters in the series of identifying numbers and letters are an abbreviation for the legal reference that contains the law or case. For example, "L.W." stands for *United States Law Week.* (To find out what the abbreviation in the citation stands for, see the list of common legal references on pages 111 and 112.)

The number that precedes the abbreviation indicates either a volume number or title classification within the legal reference. A title classification is a body of laws or cases on a particular subject, such as malpractice. A title can be one book or many books, depending on the number of cases that bear on the titles.

For a law, one set of numbers follows the abbreviation. These numbers indicate the section within the reference volume or title in which the law can be found.

For a court case, two sets of numbers follow the abbreviation. The first set indicates the page where the case can be found. The second set, in parentheses, indicates the year of the decision.

Sometimes, a court case on the state level will have two complete series of identifying numbers. The first series is the *official citation,* indicating where the case can be found in that state's set of court case decisions. The second series is the *unofficial citation,* indicating where the case can be found in a commercially published set of court case decisions grouped by region. These regional sets are explained in the listing on page 112. If the case citation only quotes the regional (commercial) listing, then the state court that heard the case, such as the Pennsylvania Commonwealth Court, is included in the parentheses with the date of the case.

## INTERPRETING LEGAL CITATIONS continued

| TYPE OF LAW OR CASE | LEGAL REFERENCE | ABBREVIATION |
|---|---|---|
| **Federal statutes** | *United States Law Week* (contains chronologic list of recently enacted statutes) | L.W. |
| | *United States Statutes at Large* (contains chronologic lists of all statutes enacted during a single legislative session) | STAT. or STAT. AT L. |
| | *United States Code* (contains all statutes arranged by title) | U.S.C. |
| **State statutes** | All states publish state statutes in official state sets | Standard state abbreviations |
| **Federal regulations** | *Code of Federal Regulations* (contains federal regulations arranged by title) | C.F.R. |
| | *The Federal Register* (contains updates to the C.F.R.) | F.R. |
| **State regulations** | All states publish state regulations in official state sets | Standard state abbreviations |
| **Federal court decisions** | *United States Law Week* (contains recently issued unofficial Supreme Court decisions) | L.W. |
| | *United States Reports* (contains official federal court decisions) | U.S. |
| | *Supreme Court Reporter* (contains official Supreme Court decisions) | S.Ct. |
| | *Lawyers Edition, United States Supreme Court* (contains official Supreme Court decisions) | L.Ed. |
| | *Federal Reporter* (contains court of appeals decisions) | F. |
| | *Federal Supplement Series* (contains Federal District Court of Appeals decisions) | F. Supp. |

continued

## INTERPRETING LEGAL CITATIONS continued

| TYPE OF LAW OR CASE | LEGAL REFERENCE | ABBREVIATION |
|---|---|---|
| State court decisions | About two-thirds of the states publish state court decisions in official state sets | Standard state abbreviations |
| | All states are included in the commercially published National Reporter System, which groups state court decisions by region: | |
| | *North Eastern Reporter* | N.E. |
| | *Atlantic Reporter* | A. |
| | *South Eastern Reporter* | S.E. |
| | *Southern Reporter* | So. |
| | *North Western Reporter* | N.W. |
| | *South Western Reporter* | S.W. |
| | *Pacific Reporter* | P. |

# Appendix F

## CANADIAN NURSES ASSOCIATION'S PROVINCIAL AND TERRITORIAL MEMBERS

**Registered Nurses Association of British Columbia**
2855 Arbutus St.
Vancouver, British Columbia V6J 3Y8

**Alberta Association of Registered Nurses**
11620-168 St.
Edmonton, Alberta T5M 4A6

**Saskatchewan Registered Nurses Association**
2066 Retallack St.
Regina, Saskatchewan S4T 2K2

**Manitoba Association of Registered Nurses**
647 Broadway
Winnipeg, Manitoba R3C 0X2

**Registered Nurses Association of Ontario**
33 Price St.
Toronto, Ontario M4W 1Z2

For information on registration and licensure in Ontario, contact:
**College of Nurses of Ontario**
101 Davenport Rd.
Toronto, Ontario M5R 3P1

**Nurses Association of New Brunswick**
231 Saunders St.
Fredericton, New Brunswick E3B 1N6

**Registered Nurses Association of Nova Scotia**
6035 Coburg Rd.
Halifax, Nova Scotia B3H 1Y8

**Association of Registered Nurses of Prince Edward Island**
P.O. Box 1838
Charlottetown, P.E.I. C1A 7N5

**Association of Registered Nurses of Newfoundland**
55 Military Rd.
Box 6116,
St. John's , NFLD A1C 5X8

**Northwest Territories Registered Nurses Association**
Box 2757
Yellowknife, Northwest Territories X1A 2R1

**Yukon Nurses Society**
Box 5371
Whitehorse, Yukon Y1A 4Z2

For information on registration and licensure in Quebec, contact:
**L'Ordre des infirmières et infirmiers du Québec**
4200 ouest, boul. Dorchester
Montréal (Québec) H3Z 1V4

# Appendix G

## JOINT COMMISSION ON ACCREDITATION OF HEALTHCARE ORGANIZATIONS NURSING CARE STANDARDS

Beginning January 1, 1991, new nursing care standards established by the JCAHO will be in effect. These standards—designed to objectively evaluate and continuously monitor the institution's overall clinical and organizational performance—apply to all settings in which nursing care is provided in the hospital.

### STANDARD

NC.1     Patients receive nursing care based on a documented assessment of their needs.

### REQUIRED CHARACTERISTICS

NC.1.1     Each patient's need for nursing care related to his admission is assessed by a registered nurse.

NC.1.1.1 The assessment is conducted either at the time of admission or within a time frame preceding or following admission that is specified in hospital policy.

NC.1.1.2 Aspects of data collection may be delegated by the registered nurse.

NC.1.1.3 Needs are reassessed when warranted by the patient's condition.

NC.1.2     Each patient's assessment includes consideration of biophysical, psychosocial, environmental, self-care, educational, and discharge planning factors.

NC.1.2.1 When appropriate, data from the patient's significant other(s) are included in the assessment.

NC.1.3     Each patient's nursing care is based on identified nursing diagnoses or patient care needs and patient care standards, and is consistent with the therapies of other disciplines.

NC.1.3.1 The patient and significant other(s) are involved in the patient's care, as appropriate.

NC.1.3.2 Nursing staff members collaborate, as appropriate, with physicians and other clinical disciplines in making decisions regarding each patient's need for nursing care.

NC.1.3.3 Throughout the patient's stay, the patient and, as appropriate, his significant other(s) receive education specific to the patient's health care needs.

NC.1.3.3.1 In preparation for discharge, continuing care needs are assessed and referrals for such care are documented in the patient's medical record.

NC.1.3.4 The patient's medical record includes documentation of:

NC.1.3.4.1 the initial assessments and reassessments

NC.1.3.4.2 the nursing diagnoses and patient care needs

NC.1.3.4.3 the interventions identified to meet the patient's nursing care needs

NC.1.3.4.4 the nursing care provided

NC.1.3.4.5 the patient's response to, and the outcome of, the care provided

NC.1.3.4.6 the abilities of the patient and significant other(s) to manage continuing care needs after discharge.

**JOINT COMMISSION ON ACCREDITATION OF HEALTHCARE ORGANIZATIONS NURSING CARE STANDARDS** continued

NC.1.3.5 Nursing care data related to patient assessments, the nursing care planned, nursing interventions, and patient outcomes are permanently integrated into the clinical information system (for example, the medical record).

NC.1.3.5.1 Nursing care data can be identified and retrieved from the clinical information system.

## STANDARD

NC.2    All members of the nursing staff are competent to fulfill their assigned responsibilities.

## REQUIRED CHARACTERISTICS

NC.2.1    Each member of the nursing staff is assigned clinical or managerial responsibilities based on educational preparation, applicable licensing laws and regulations, and an assessment of current competence.

NC.2.1.1 An evaluation of each nursing staff member's competence is conducted at defined intervals throughout the individual's association with the hospital.

NC.2.1.1.1 The evaluation includes an objective assessment of the individual's performance in delivering patient care services in accordance with patient needs.

NC.2.1.1.2 The process for evaluating competence is defined in policy and procedure.

NC.2.1.2 Nursing care responsibilities are assigned to a nursing staff member in accordance with:

NC.2.1.2.1 the degree of supervision needed by the individual and its availability

NC.2.1.2.2 the complexity and dynamics of the condition of each patient to whom the individual is to provide services and the complexity of the assessment required by each patient, including:

NC.2.1.2.2.1 the factors that must be considered to make appropriate decisions regarding the provision of nursing care

NC.2.1.2.2.2 the type of technology employed in providing nursing care.

NC.2.2    The determination of a nursing staff member's current clinical competence and the assignment of nursing care responsibilities are the responsibility of registered nurses who have the clinical and managerial knowledge and experience necessary to competently make these decisions.

NC.2.3    Nursing staff members participate in orientation, regularly scheduled staff meetings, and ongoing education designed to improve their competence.

NC.2.3.1 Participation is documented.

NC.2.3.2 Appropriate nursing staff members demonstrate competence in cardiopulmonary resuscitation and other patient safety areas as defined by hospital policy.

continued

**JOINT COMMISSION ON ACCREDITATION OF HEALTHCARE ORGANIZATIONS NURSING CARE STANDARDS** continued

**NC.2.3.2.1** Competence of these nursing staff members is demonstrated and documented at least every two years.

**NC.2.3.3** If a nursing staff member is assigned to more than one type of nursing unit or patient, the staff member is competent to provide nursing care to patients in each unit and to each type of patient.

**NC.2.3.3.1** Adequate and timely orientation and cross-training are provided as needed.

**NC.2.4** If the hospital uses outside sources for nursing personnel, these personnel receive orientation before providing patient care.

**NC.2.4.1** Documented evidence of licensure and current clinical competence in assigned patient care responsibilities is reviewed and approved by the hospital before these nursing personnel engage in patient care activities.

**NC.2.4.1.1** The performance of these nursing personnel in the hospital is evaluated.

**NC.2.4.1.1.1** Responsibility for this evaluation is defined in hospital policy.

## STANDARD
**NC.3** The nurse executive and other appropriate registered nurses develop hospitalwide patient care programs, policies, and procedures that describe how the nursing care needs of patients or patient populations are assessed, evaluated, and met.

## REQUIRED CHARACTERISTICS
**NC.3.1** Policies and procedures, based on nursing standards of patient care and standards of nursing practice, describe and guide the nursing care provided.

**NC.3.1.1** The nurse executive has the authority and responsibility for establishing standards of nursing practice.

**NC.3.1.2** The policies, procedures, nursing standards of patient care, and standards of nursing practice are:

**NC.3.1.2.1** developed by the nurse executive, registered nurses, and other designated nursing staff members

**NC.3.1.2.2** defined in writing

**NC.3.1.2.3** approved by the nurse executive or a designee

**NC.3.1.2.4** used, as indicated, in the assessment of the quality of patient care

**NC.3.1.2.5** reviewed and modified whenever warranted.

**NC.3.1.2.5.1** Nursing policy establishes a minimum period between reviews, not to exceed three years.

**NC.3.1.2.5.2** The review includes information about the relevance of policies, procedures, nursing standards of patient care, and standards of nursing practice in actual use; ethical and legal concerns; current scientific knowledge; and findings from quality assurance and other evaluation mechanisms, as appropriate.

**JOINT COMMISSION ON ACCREDITATION OF HEALTHCARE ORGANIZATIONS NURSING CARE STANDARDS** continued

**NC.3.2**  Nursing staff members have a defined mechanism for addressing ethical issues in patient care.

**NC.3.2.1** When the hospital has an ethics committee or other defined structures for addressing ethical issues in patient care, nursing staff members participate.

**NC.3.3**  Policies and procedures are developed in collaboration with other clinical and administrative groups, when appropriate.

**NC.3.3.1** The nurse executive, or a designee, participates in the hospital admissions system to coordinate patient requirements for nursing care with available nursing resources.

**NC.3.3.1.1** In making the decision when or where to admit or transfer a patient, consideration is given to the ability of the nursing staff to assess and meet the patient's nursing care needs.

**NC.3.4**  Policies and procedures describe the mechanism used to assign nursing staff members to meet patient care needs.

**NC.3.4.1** There are sufficient qualified nursing staff members to meet the nursing care needs of patients throughout the hospital.

**NC.3.4.1.1** The criteria for employment, deployment, and assignment of nursing staff members are approved by the nurse executive.

**NC.3.4.2** Nurse staffing plans for each unit define the number and mix of nursing personnel in accordance with current patient care needs.

**NC.3.4.2.1** In designing and assessing nurse staffing plans, the hospital gives appropriate consideration to the utilization of registered nurses, licensed practical/vocational nurses, nursing assistants, and other nursing personnel, and to the potential contribution these personnel can make to the delivery of efficient and effective patient care.

**NC.3.4.2.2** The staffing schedules are reviewed and adjusted as necessary to meet defined patient needs and unusual occurrences.

**NC.3.4.2.3** Appropriate and sufficient support services are available to allow nursing staff members to meet the nursing care needs of patients and their significant other(s).

**NC.3.4.2.4.** Staffing levels are adequate to support participation of nursing staff members, as assigned, in committees and meetings and in quality assurance and educational activities.

## STANDARD
**NC.4**  The hospital's plan for providing nursing care is designed to support improvement and innovation in nursing practice and is based on both the needs of the patients to be served and the hospital's mission.

## REQUIRED CHARACTERISTICS
**NC.4.1**  The plan for nurse staffing and the provision of nursing care is reviewed in detail on an annual basis and receives periodic attention as warranted by changing patient care needs and outcomes.

continued

**JOINT COMMISSION ON ACCREDITATION OF HEALTHCARE ORGANIZATIONS NURSING CARE STANDARDS** continued

**NC.4.1.1** Registered nurses prescribe, delegate, and coordinate the nursing care provided throughout the hospital.

**NC.4.1.2** Consistent standards for the provision of nursing care within the hospital are used to monitor and evaluate the quality and appropriateness of nursing care provided throughout the hospital.

**NC.4.2** The appropriateness of the hospital's plan for providing nursing care to meet patient needs is reviewed as part of the established budget review process.

**NC.4.2.1** The review includes:

**NC.4.2.1.1** an analysis of actual staffing patterns

**NC.4.2.1.2** findings from quality assurance activities.

**NC.4.2.2** The allocation of financial and other resources is assessed to determine whether nursing care is provided appropriately, efficiently, and effectively.

**NC.4.2.2.1** The allocation of financial and other resources is designed to support improvement and innovation in nursing practice.

## STANDARD
**NC.5** The nurse executive and other nursing leaders participate with leaders from the governing body, management, medical staff, and clinical areas in the hospital's decision-making structures and processes.

## REQUIRED CHARACTERISTICS
**NC.5.1** Nursing services are directed by a nurse executive who is a registered nurse qualified by advanced education and management experience.

**NC.5.1.1** If the hospital utilizes a decentralized organizational structure, there is an identified nurse leader at the executive level to provide authority and accountability for, and coordination of, the nurse executive functions.

**NC.5.1.2** When the hospital is part of a multihospital system, there is a mechanism for the hospital's nurse executive to participate in policy decisions affecting patient care services at relevant levels of corporate decision making within the system.

**NC.5.1.2.1** The mechanism is used to enhance the exchange of information about, as well as participation in, improving the nursing care provided to patients in the hospital.

**NC.5.1.2.2** The mechanism is defined in writing.

**NC.5.2** The nurse executive, or a designee, participates with leaders from the governing body, management, medical staff, and clinical areas in developing the hospital's mission, strategic plans, budgets, resource allocation, operation plans, and policies.

**NC.5.2.1** The nurse executive develops the nursing budget in collaboration with other nursing leaders and other hospital personnel.

## JOINT COMMISSION ON ACCREDITATION OF HEALTHCARE ORGANIZATIONS NURSING CARE STANDARDS continued

**NC.5.2.2** The nurse executive and other nursing leaders participate in the ongoing review of the hospital's mission, strategic plans, and policies.

**NC.5.3** The nurse executive and other nursing leaders participate with leaders from the governing body, management, medical staff, and clinical areas in planning, promoting, and conducting hospitalwide quality monitoring and improvement activities.

**NC.5.3.1** Registered nurses evaluate current nursing practice and patient care delivery models to improve the quality, appropriateness, and efficiency of patient care.

**NC.5.3.2** The nurse executive and other nursing leaders participate in developing and implementing mechanisms for collaboration between nursing staff members, physicians, and other clinical practitioners.

**NC.5.4** The nurse executive and other nursing leaders are responsible for developing, implementing, and evaluating programs to promote the recruitment, retention, development, and continuing education of nursing staff members.

**NC.5.4.1** The nurse executive and other nursing leaders participate in developing and implementing mechanisms for recognizing the expertise and performance of nursing staff members engaged in patient care.

**NC.5.4.2** The nurse executive and other nursing leaders collaborate with governing body and other management and clinical leaders to develop mechanisms for promoting the educational and advancement goals of hospital staff members.

**NC.5.5** The nurse executive, or a designee, participates in evaluating, selecting, and integrating health care technology and information management systems that support patient care needs and the efficient utilization of nursing resources.

**NC.5.5.1** The use of efficient interactive information management systems for nursing, other clinical (for example, dietary, pharmacy, physical therapy), and nonclinical information is facilitated wherever appropriate.

**NC.5.6** When the hospital provides clinical facilities for nursing education programs, appropriate nursing leaders collaborate with nursing educators to influence curricula, including clinical and managerial learning experiences.

## STANDARD

**NC.6** As part of the hospital's quality assurance program, the quality and appropriateness of the patient care provided by all members of the nursing staff are monitored and evaluated.

## REQUIRED CHARACTERISTICS

**NC.6.1** The nurse executive is responsible for implementing the monitoring and evaluation process.

**NC.6.1.1** Nursing staff members participate in:

**NC.6.1.1.1** the identification of the important aspects of care for each patient care unit

continued

**JOINT COMMISSION ON ACCREDITATION OF HEALTHCARE ORGANIZATIONS NURSING CARE STANDARDS** continued

**NC.6.1.1.2** the identification of the indicators used to monitor the quality and appropriateness of the important aspects of care

**NC.6.1.1.3** the evaluation of the quality and appropriateness of care.

**NC.6.2**    When an outside source provides nursing services, the nurse executive, or the chief executive officer in the absence of a nurse executive, is responsible for implementing the monitoring and evaluation process.

Reprinted with permission from JCAHO.

# Index

t refers to a table

# Notes